SOCIAL SCIENCES DIVISION
CHICAGO PUBLIC LIBRARY
400 SOUTH STATE STREET
CHICAGO, IL 60605

DISCARD

D0651981

DISCARD

CREED OF A CONGRESSMAN

Creed of a Congressman
F. EDWARD HÉBERT OF LOUISIANA

Edited and Evaluated
by
GLENN R. CONRAD
with a
Biographical Sketch
by
VIRGINEA R. BURGUIÈRES

Published by
THE USL HISTORY SERIES
The University of Southwestern Louisiana
Lafayette, Louisiana
1970

E
748
H 3895
.C6 c

Soc,

Library of Congress Catalog Card Number 70–633180

COPYRIGHT © 1971 BY THE UNIVERSITY OF SOUTHWESTERN
LOUISIANA, LAFAYETTE, LOUISIANA, ALL RIGHTS RESERVED.

FIRST EDITION

Manufactured in the United States of America by
The TJM Corporation, Baton Rouge, Louisiana.

THE CHICAGO PUBLIC LIBRARY
MAY - 6 '72 B

SOC

DISCARD
SOCIAL SCIENCES DIVISION
CHICAGO PUBLIC LIBRARY
400 SOUTH STATE STREET
CHICAGO, IL 60605

5.95

DISCARD

PORTRAIT OF A STATESMAN

The only portrait of a living person hanging in the Presbytere of the Louisiana State Museum close by the Cabildo at Jackson Square, where the transfer of the Territory of Louisiana to the United States from France took place in 1803, is that of F. Edward Hebert. Facing this page is a photograph of that portrait. The legend affixed to it reads:

F. EDWARD HEBERT

Newspaperman—Congressman

Born October 12, 1901. Son of Lea Naquin and Felix J. Hebert; Husband of Gladys Bofill, Father of Dawn Marie (Mrs. John Malcolm Duhe, Jr.), Grandfather of Kim Marie, Jeanne Louise, Edward Malcolm, and Martin Bofill Duhe.

Entered the United States House of Representatives on January 3, 1941, as a Member of Congress from the First Congressional District of Louisiana. On January 3, 1966, became the first individual in the history of the State of Louisiana to serve for twenty-five consecutive years, a quarter of a century, in the United States House of Representatives.

THE PORTRAIT

by John Clay Parker

In this life-size portrait, I have attempted to vividly capture the personality and character of Congressman Hebert and have surrounded him with the most important symbols of his colorful life and career.

To the right in the background is the United States Capitol in Washington, where Congressman Hebert began his service in 1941. In the lower right-hand corner is a world globe bringing to mind his world travels as a member of the Armed Services Committee. At the upper left are the three flags under which the Congressman serves—the American, the State of Louisiana and the City of New Orleans.

On the desk are the gavel, symbol of authority as chairman over the many committees in Congress which he has headed; the cannon symbolic of his close association with the armed services in peace and war; the quill recalling Congressman Hebert's writings as a reporter and newspaperman, and finally, the bust of the Greek orator Demosthenes, suggesting Congressman Hebert's reputation as a forceful and dynamic orator and speaker.

The book being held by Congressman Hebert is a copy of "I Went, I Saw, I Heard" which he wrote upon his return from war-torn Europe in 1945. The Cathedral of Rheims is easily discernible on the back cover. The Hebert Coat of Arms can easily be seen engraved on the ring he is wearing . . . a gift to him at a testimonial dinner in 1962, and which is inscribed "To F. Edward Hebert from a grateful people."

The size of the canvas is 88 inches by 52 inches exclusive of the goldleaf frame.

DISCARD

To my parents:
Julian and Margaret Conrad

DISCARD

. . . As I look back now over the many, many years that I've been in Congress, . . . I find that I haven't changed my ideals. I find that I haven't changed my position. I find that the things I said and wrote thirty years ago could be read today without changing a line, without removing a comma or crossing another "t." I take a certain pride in that consistency.

—F. Edward Hébert, M.C., July 28, 1968

TABLE OF CONTENTS DISCARD

DISCARD

T HIS WORK SEEKS to investigate, at least partially, the political philosophy of a congressman to determine what part, if any, is played by a man's personal creed in producing the career representative in our national Congress. This study is not an effort to analyze the election of the two-year congressional phenomenon, but rather it is an attempt to gain some insight into the career of a man who has served his district for thirty years and today (1970) is the tenth ranking member of the House of Representatives. The man is F. Edward Hebert of Louisiana's First Congressional District.

In the making of a congressman, the factors are many that combine to produce the successful aspirant to the legislative chamber of this nation—and perhaps that is a reflection of the age in which we live. In today's society of multiple interests, it is difficult for a would-be representative to promote a single issue in order to be elected. Almost without exception, a candidate must display a knowledge, although completely general in tone, of the major foreign and domestic issues currently confronting America.

But as the successful representative will readily attest, one is required to have considerably more than a superficial knowledge of current issues to win election. Additional factors, such as organization, financial backing, the candidate's sincerity and appearance, to name but a few, are equally important. The combination of these ingredients, however, does not always insure election —the result can also be disappointment and defeat. Furthermore, the combination of the necessary ingredients for election may prove successful at one time thus producing the sweetness of victory, and yet, within two, four, or six years, these same ingredients may only produce the gall of defeat.

F. Edward Hebert has been a successful candidate and a successful representative for thirty years. On sixteen occasions he has gone to his constituents and asked for their confidence in his ability to represent them in Congress. On sixteen occasions the people of New Orleans, St. Bernard and Plaquemines parishes have given their representative the nod. Why?

The answer to that question becomes the focal point of this work. In all fairness, however, to the subject of this investigation and to the reader, the author does not intend to scrutinize each minute factor that has contributed to making Mr. Hebert one of the leading congressmen of our times. For example, the author will not attempt to come to grips with each political issue of the last thirty years that has interested Hebert, for to do so would be to engage in a monotonous recital of issues long forgotten or subsequently amended. Instead, the first chapter will present a biographical sketch of F. Edward Hebert. The function of this chapter is to acquaint the reader with the environmental factors of the subject's life—factors which have definitely affected the political philosophy of the Congressman. Chapters II, III and IV are devoted to an analysis of Mr. Hebert's congressional career through a general investigation of his political philosophy as reflected in his speeches, radio and television addresses, and correspondence of the past thirty years. In this way the author seeks to demonstrate some of the factors that have led to the successful congressional career of this Louisianian.

Researching his speeches and correspondence of the last three decades, one discovers that Eddie Hebert is not the stereotyped politician. He definitely cannot be classified as one of those institutions of self-perpetuation who manage to get themselves elected to Congress every two years because it has become a local or personal tradition. There is a difference, a decided difference, to be found in this man from New Orleans. His spirit of individualism, independence and confidence in America is reminiscent of the early days of the Republic. In an age when Janus-faced politicians have become accepted as the "mod look," Hebert's down-to-earth philosophy of politics, his character and his sincerity are as refreshing as a crisp autumn day. Furthermore, one discovers in Hebert's speeches and correspondence an adherence to fundamental beliefs in what America is and what it ought to be. This train of thinking, arising from principles upon which this country was founded, dominates the man's career and remains as constant as the inherent rights of mankind. Indeed, the key thread in the fabric of Hebert's congressional career can be summed up in one word—consistency. The man's public utterances demonstrate an unyielding dedication to the concepts that have made America a great nation. Thus, whether in public or in the solitude of his congressional office, Mr. Hebert has but one commitment—service to America. This commitment, in turn, has resulted in his devotion to independence of action, nonpartisan posture in the House of Representatives, and responsible individualism. Mr. Hebert has said on numerous occasions that loyalty to his beliefs is the greatest virtue a man can possess. This thought becomes increasingly impressive as one discovers the high plane upon which this Louisianian has built and maintained his ethical code.

The author has prevailed upon Virginea Burguières to prepare the biographical sketch of F. Edward Hebert. The selection of Mrs. Burguières was founded upon several factors. Primarily, however, she was selected because of the kinship of her professional background in journalism and politics with similar aspects of Hebert's career.

Mrs. Burguières began her career as a reporter and columnist for the *New Orleans Item*. In this way and through her associates she became familiar with the work of another reporter of an earlier day, the Congressman from Louisiana's First District, F. Edward Hebert.

Then, in the course of events, Virginea was thrust into the world of politics when she accepted a position as secretary to Councilman-at-Large Victor H. Schiro. Subsequently, she served as Mr. Schiro's secretary during his first term as mayor of New Orleans.

As secretary to the mayor of one of the nation's largest cities, Virginea became involved with the inner workings and behind-the-scenes aspects of politics. Thus she had official contact on a political and governmental level with the former reporter who represents Louisiana's First Congressional District in the Congress of the United States.

In time, Mrs. Burguières accepted a position as Executive Secretary to Mr. Hebert, in charge of his district office in New Orleans. From that vantage point Virginea has had the opportunity to gain a firsthand knowledge of the Congressman's life and career.

It is with considerable appreciation that the author acknowledges Mrs. Burguières' contribution to this work.

The author also takes this opportunity to express gratitude to Mr. and Mrs. John M. Duhe, Jr., the "librarians" of the F. Edward Hebert library in New Iberia, Louisiana. Both John and Dawn have cooperated with the author in various areas of research and discussion. Their assistance has been invaluable.

The author is particularly indebted to Miss Flossie Montgomery who, in her spare time, read the manuscript and suggested alterations. One is fortunate indeed to be associated with a person so completely devoted to scholarship.

Last, but most importantly, let me acknowledge my thanks to William G. Helis, Jr., whose encouragement and guidance made this work possible.

New Iberia, Louisiana   GLENN R. CONRAD
April, 1970

I FIRST MET United States Representative F. Edward Hebert in the middle of the Mississippi River at New Orleans.

It was early May of 1962. The occasion was an old-fashioned riverboat parade on the steamer *President*, celebrating the first full term inauguration of Victor H. Schiro as Mayor of the City of New Orleans. I was to be the new mayor's personal secretary. But as a former newspaperwoman on the old *New Orleans Item*, my interest in the fourth estate remained keen and constant.

It was at the *New Orleans Item* that I first heard about a legendary reporter named Eddie Hebert. I had heard old-timers bemoan the thinning ranks of those hard-fighting and hard-drinking men of yesteryear to whom the end fully justified whatever means employed to get a story. I had heard of the determined, sometimes cocky, often flamboyant Eddie Hebert who came up through the ranks to the top of his profession when he became city editor of the *New Orleans States*. I had heard of this reporter who had colorfully recorded those convulsive years in Louisiana's history during the 1930's—the era that produced a political phenomenon named Huey P. Long. I had heard of the city editor who broke the story of the Louisiana Scandals that led to the collapse of as powerful a political machine as the country had ever known.

So this is Eddie Hebert, I remember thinking to myself as I acknowledged the introduction on the upper deck of the steamer *President* that day on the Mississippi.

I beheld a towering figure, well over six feet, immaculate in a

well-tailored white suit and with the alert countenance of an eagle.
This was the legendary reporter turned editor who stood before
me now as the United States Representative from Louisiana's First
Congressional District—an office he has held effortlessly since
1941, when he decided to stop reporting the news and began making news by defeating the ten-year incumbent in a two to one victory for a seat in the 77th Congress of the United States.

On January 1, 1966, four years after my riverboat meeting, I
became a member of Congressman Hebert's Congressional staff.
I was appointed Executive Secretary to the Congressman in charge
of his District Office in New Orleans.

This biographical sketch is not intended as a thorough, in-depth
study of the life of F. Edward Hebert. That will be left to his-
torians.

Chapter I is presented as a capsule chronicle of the man's life,
with occasional expansion, and is an attempt to trace and portray
for the reader the interlocking levels of Hebert's life that blended
to produce this gentleman from Louisiana who twice in his own
lifetime has become a legend.

This will also be an attempt to provide the reader with a close-
at-hand view of the early and unchanging qualities and philosophies that guided and motivated Eddie Hebert from boyhood to
manhood and produced the subject matter of this book which
Glenn Conrad has authored.

New Orleans, Louisiana   VIRGINEA R. BURGUIÈRES
April, 1970

CREED OF A CONGRESSMAN

BIOGRAPHICAL SKETCH

T HE BOY . . . at the Beginning . . .

Felix Edward Hebert was born in New Orleans on famed Canal Street. He was the first of two sons born to Lea Naquin and Felix J. Hebert. The second son and only other child was Gordon Roy Hebert.

Hebert's early education was in the public and parochial schools of New Orleans. Miss Felicie Pollet, who taught him from the third to the sixth grade, is still alive and remembers young Eddie Hebert well. She had this to say about the boy she taught more than fifty years ago:

> He never did directly object to anything during those years I taught him. But he always had another way of reaching it or telling about it. So, one day he handed me two sheets of paper with a bill . . . the way Congress writes a bill . . . and he was the Speaker of the House. The class had gotten together and formed committees and they were opposing some of those things I had demanded of them in the classroom. He presented it to me, to accept or veto, as though I were the President. And it was well written; he had copied from the *Book of Knowledge* or something like that because it was written the way a bill in Congress is written.[1]

Miss Pollet also recalled another incident with young Eddie Hebert—an incident that foreshadowed his determination to reach an objective. Eddie Hebert had asked Miss Pollet what he had to do to receive an "E" on his report card in deportment.

Well, on the spur of the moment I said, 'You can't open your mouth once for a whole month.' He said, 'All right, I promise you I won't open my mouth.' During the whole month I watched him like a hawk. I could see when the boys pulled on his shirt and things to make him talk, and they would ask him something to make him talk, but he would shrug his shoulders and not talk. And I watched him, but I didn't see him break his promise, so I had to give him an "E" in deportment! And it was hard for him, because he was always in some devilment— not any badness—but always up to something interesting that applied to what was going on at the time.[2]

At St. Joseph's Parochial School, Eddie Hebert decided one day the school needed a newspaper. With nothing to guide him but instinct, he produced a dummy sheet for a complete front page layout. Although the terms "dummy", "make-up", and "layout" were strangers to his youthful vocabulary, Hebert recalled that years later when he became city editor of the *New Orleans States*, he never made a better or fundamentally more perfect "layout" than that early attempt. However, he also recalled that his youthful ambition to become a publisher, as well as a reporter, was shattered when the printer told him it would cost a whopping $9 to print just one edition!

Hebert's secondary schooling was at Jesuit High School in New Orleans. There began a love affair between a boy and a school that has grown and deepened with the passing years. Second only to his mother, Hebert gives full and unrestrained credit to the Jesuits for their molding and shaping of the boy to manhood.

It was during his Jesuit days that the relentless and driving personality of Eddie Hebert began to take definite form and pattern. A tall, gangling boy, he was unable to participate in contact sports. He wore glasses and had lost the sight in his left eye in a childhood accident. To a devoted sports fan like Hebert, this limitation was a deep disappointment, but one for which he soon compensated by becoming manager of all the athletic teams at Jesuit.

Competition emerged as the fire that fed Eddie Hebert's drive. But it was not the competition of scholastics that inspired him. It was people competition. The challenge of oratory and debate spurred him on to win every elocution and debating award offered at Jesuit. His willful determination and oratorical persuasion resulted in his election to class president during his junior and senior years.

One of Hebert's most prophetic debates at Jesuit High, for which he was named "Best Orator," took place on Saturday, June 16, 1916. With life's future pages blank and uncharted, it can be said that on that day he made a date with destiny—a date which he kept—fifty years later.

The subject for debate was: "Resolved: That Military Instruction in High Schools Should be a Compulsory Part of Education." Eddie Hebert was fifteen years old. He debated the affirmative side. Here, in his own words and as he wrote it, is Hebert's debate:

Father Moderator, Officers, Members of the Philalethic Society, my colleague has proved to you that military training in high schools is beneficial from a physical and moral standpoint. I will try to prove it beneficial in times of war.

Let us glance at the condition of the United States at the beginning of the present trouble with Mexico. Of the citizens that applied for service in the militia, 80% were turned down, they not being fit for military service of any kind. The cause of this sad plight was that they had never been trained before. On the other hand, if each had had from three to four years training while still attending school, he would have been ready to fall promptly into line and defend this grand old United States which Washington and our forefathers helped make.

The peril of being unprepared to put trained citizens into the field of battle on short notice has been sounded by military men and statesmen from the time of Washington. To send our men untrained into war to meet equally good men, well trained and disciplined, was once described by Light Horse Harry Lee of Revolutionary fame as murder. This perhaps is too strong, but it is certainly a gross disregard for human life.

There is a little poem which goes on to say, that when England loses men she does not care; when France loses men she thinks it unfair; but when Germany loses men she puts more in their place. Why is it that Germany can put more men in line? I ask why? It is because her men were trained while attending school. And look what Germany has been doing for the last two and a half years. She has been holding the combined powers of England, France, Russia and other countries at bay. She could not have done this if her citizens had not been trained while still attending school. If Germany does this in its schools, why can't our own grand and nobler United States do the same?

In a letter to President Monroe, Thomas Jefferson advocated compulsory military service in the following words, 'We must train and classify the whole of our male citizens and make military instruction a part of collegiate education.'

The principle laid down in this message is just as sound today as it was when uttered more than 75 years ago, and it is even more pertinent in all which relates to a reasonable degree of preparedness as war comes more quickly now.

We can go back to the time when Greece and Sparta were at their height among the world's powers. The first thing a Grecian or Spartan thought of was to prepare himself for the defense of his country which was the dearest thing to his heart. If other countries do and have done this, why can't we?

The United States Army is an organization of a few thousand professional soldiers backed by the manhood of the country—untrained. Why is this manhood untrained? You gentlemen who are the rising generation—it is for you to see that this manhood is trained.

During the summer of 1913, two military camps for the instruction of students were established and became highly successful. Why not continue this good work in the high schools of the United States?

In conclusion, I ask you gentlemen, also my honorable opponents, to picture this grand old city of New Orleans, your city and my city, the metropolis of the South, laid in ruins by a hostile fleet. Picture your mother, your father or your sister, slain by an enemy's hand. All because you were untrained and not fit to defend your home and your country.

What shall future America be, gentlemen? Her fate is in your hands. Shall we be defenseless America, a weak and harmless nation, or shall we be defensive America, the fear and dread of all nations? [3]

On May 16, 1966, fifty years after that debate was delivered, I had the rare privilege of being witness to one of Congressman F. Edward Hebert's proudest moments. I saw him stand at attention, head held high, alongside General Wallace M. Greene, Jr., Commandant of the United States Marine Corps, and on the Jesuit High School parade grounds, review the first Junior ROTC unit in the nation to be activated. This was accomplished through Eddie Hebert's efforts and dogged determination.

I saw Eddie Hebert keep a date with destiny—made fifty years ago—and complete a sentimental journey on the grounds of his beloved Jesuit High School.

The Patriotic Student—Reporter—City Editor

Eddie Hebert's fierce love of country is deeply mingled with his strong feeling that an obligation is owed by the present generation to the dead heroes of the past—an obligation to hold high and burning the torch of freedom tossed by others from the pages of history. And so it was that Eddie Hebert the patriot emerged during high school years. It was to be the same brand of patriotism that guided him to the halls of Congress and to which he has subsequently held steadfast.

In 1918, six months before the end of World War I, Eddie Hebert was seventeen years old. He wrote the following essay under the title "Patriotism."

> Patriotism is love of country and is a virtue which next to love of God is the most essential thing to man. It is a virtue which comes from the heart and is not merely an exterior devotion. Patriotism cannot be bought and sold like slaves on the auction block to the highest bidder; it must be infused into our hearts by God. A man once possessed of the proper patriotism is always a patriot. Love of country is born like innocence into everyone's heart; but if we do not take the proper care of keeping this love, it will slip through our fingers.

Patriotism may be displayed in peace or in war; it may be displayed by man, woman or child. In peace the real patriot shows the true blue blood circulating in his veins by giving proper attention to the welfare and progress of his country.

In war he is still better able to display his real colors. It is not necessary for one to distinguish himself on the shell-torn battlefields by some heroic deed, to be a patriot. There are some who never smell powder; who never are exposed to shell fire; who never have heard the command, 'Over the Top,' still among these are found some of the staunchest and the truest patriots. Not every man displays patriotism in the same manner. Take this great World War for instance. We are sending the flower of our manhood 'Over There' to sacrifice their lives if need be, in order to uphold Democracy and a great nation's honor on the blood-stained fields of France. These defenders of liberty, freedom and justice are one set of patriots. Now we have the co-patriots of these noble fighters, the ones who stay at home and who are the support behind the man behind the gun.

The mother who gives her son up to her country is as true a patriot as the man who sacrifices his life on the field of honor. The men and the women who are not blessed with children and who are unable to fight may also prove their patriotism by financing their government in proportion to their means. Even children can be patriots. The little ones are unable to fight or to finance; but they can work war gardens and perform other minor helps. This is the second class of patriots. Remember that everyone, whether young or old, can show their patriotism by performing one of these great works—farm, finance or fight.

Foremost among our nation's patriots stands George Washington, the Father of his Country. The name of Washington is honored by the entire world. His memory is loved and cherished by the children of the great country which he helped make. Not very far behind Washington in patriotism are such men as Bishop Carroll, Benjamin Franklin, Jack Barry, Abraham Lincoln and many others.

See in what great respect these men are held in the eyes of man. Now look at the traitor Benedict Arnold, the cur who attempted to sell his country for English gold. The very name of Arnold is held in hatred and contempt by honest people.

Following Arnold is General Charles Lee, who, jealous of Washington, disclosed the plans of the American army to the British. Thank God that America has very few men of this type. Oh, would that such men had never been born than to become such wretches.

Another fine example of American patriotism is found in Captain Nathan Hale who, disguised, crossed into the British lines as a spy for the Continental forces. Unfortunately he was caught, courtmartialed and sentenced to be hanged as a spy. His last words, while standing on the gallows were, 'I am sorry that I have but one life to give for my country.'

Every true, loyal American should try to follow in the footsteps of patriotism left by some of their noble predecessors. Love of our country should be second only to the love which we owe the Supreme Being, who alone makes patriotism possible. We should all live up to the immortal words of Admirals Decatur and Dewey: 'My country, may she forever be right; but right or wrong, my country.' [4]

By the time Eddie Hebert graduated from Jesuit High School in 1920, his qualities of leadership, his success in winning elections and his gift of oratory were all on record. The political possibilities of such a 3-pronged sword were not lost on his classmates. Beneath Hebert's picture in the yearbook was inscribed the class prophecy, "Choose any office in the land and it shall be thine."

But another flame was being slowly fanned—one that was to blaze brightly and leave legendary embers before Hebert joined the hustings to fulfill his class prophecy.

Hebert was still a student at Jesuit when he became assistant sports editor for the New Orleans *Times-Picayune*, and the first sports writer in New Orleans to write exclusively on prep school sports. It was during that period he decided Jesuit athletes should have a name and that it should be Blue Jay and that their motto should be "Once a Blue Jay, Always a Blue Jay."

Hebert entered Tulane University with the push of politics and the excitement of newspaper reporting jockeying for position. Temporarily, he accommodated both. He successfully campaigned for president of the Freshman Class (next year the Sophomore Class) and was the first freshman in the history of the university to win the championship in debating. He also continued as assistant sports editor for *The Times-Picayune* and added to that the distinction of becoming the first sports editor of the school's newspaper, the Tulane *Hullabaloo*.

When Hebert left Tulane he switched his sports writing from *The Times-Picayune* to the *New Orleans States*. Added to that activity was publicity director for Loyola University, publicity for the Tulane (legitimate theatre), Orpheum and St. Charles theatres. Gradually his field of endeavor narrowed and the *New Orleans States* claimed his total talents. From promotions director he went on to general news reporting and feature writing. In 1934 he became political editor of the paper and for seven years wrote a daily, front-page column called "The Periscope." It was a Pearson-Winchell type column that took politicians apart every afternoon.

It was also a column that frequently expressed the personal philosophies and thoughts of Eddie Hebert; his great love and respect for his mother and for all mothers; his deep awareness of the past as a prologue of the future; and his stern conviction of the responsibilities of leaders to set proper examples for the generation of future leaders.

On June 9, 1935, Hebert wrote his "Periscope" column about youth and its ideals. It was prompted by the expulsion of seven senior journalism students from Louisiana State University because they rebelled against political censorship of *The Reveille*, the university newspaper. The full text of Hebert's column bears repeating:

> The greatest tragedy that can befall youth is to lose faith in its ideals. When ideals perish, life becomes a drab, meaningless existence—when ideals are shattered there is nothing that we can hope for—when our tabernacle of ideals crash we find ourselves broken in spirit—weakened in courage—clasping only to a straw of life. The loss of idealism is sad at any time in life, but its loss in youth is irreparable. The hope of a nation is embedded in the idealism of its youth. Humanity must of necessity turn to the

idealism of youth for its betterment. 'While stands the Coliseum, Rome shall stand; when falls the Coliseum, Rome shall fall; and when Rome falls—the world!' said the pilgrims of the eighth century and penned the poet. Well, could we paraphrase these lines? 'While idealism lives, youth shall live; when idealism dies, youth shall die; and when youth dies—the nation! . . .

A New York editor gained undying fame with a famous Christmas editorial in which he replied to a little girl who stood on the dangerous precipice of loss of faith in a child's Santa Claus, 'Yes, Virginia there is a Santa Claus,' he wrote in answer to the query of the little girl. And this writer painted such a beautiful and magnificent picture of the idealism of a Santa Claus that he not only restored the child's faltering faith and kept alive her ideals but he kept burning the fires of idealism in an entire nation and even to this day that editorial is quoted and reprinted. What a tragedy it would have been for even one little girl to lose her faith.

Only too short a time ago, seven youths at Louisiana State University found themselves in much the same position of the little girl to whom that famous editorial was addressed. They were expelled from their university because they fought for their ideals—because they believed in the principles of the freedom of the press and free speech, the foundation on which the structure of democracy has been built. And when one of those seven youths told a professor that he was fighting for a principle, he was told: 'When you get as old as I am you will learn that principles don't mean much!' How brutal! How inhuman! Gone was the faith of that mere stripling—shattered were his ideals—his world of idealism had fallen. What a tragedy!!! Those seven boys looked on a horizon of the future undotted with hope—barren of ideals. What had they to live for?

Is it any wonder that they found themselves doubting whether or not their fight was worth the price? Is it any wonder that they doubted whether there remained anything decent or fine in the world for which to hope. They had fought for an ideal and had been branded—they had battled for a principle and had been told that principles didn't mean much after all. They were lost in a wilderness of confusion between right and wrong when the Uni-

versity of Missouri opened wide its benevolent arms and beck-
oned them to enter its shelter. But there was another obstacle to
overcome—the obstacle of the necessary money to finance their
future education and again those seven boys wondered if those
who proclaimed ideals and principles became silent when called
to action. 'Did principles mean much after all?', they dubiously
asked.

Yes, boys, principles do mean something after all. There are
ideals and there are principles and there are men and women who
preach idealism and live up to the standards of their ideals. The
story hasn't been told yet but $1200 has been raised by an un-
named group of men and women in order to finance those boys
through Missouri—to prove to them that their fight was not in
vain. The men and women who have contributed that money are
'unwept, unhonored and unsung' because they have refused
recognition for an act which they considered merely an act of
idealism and principle. That money is not a gratuity. It is not a
gift, but a loan to boys who also possess ideals and principle. That
fund stands as a monument to idealism and principle.

Those boys today know that he who dies for an ideal is not a
lost soul. They know that, despite what one professor said, principles do count for something. They know that there are still
clean and decent things in life. They know that idealism is still
alive in the world and that there is still hope for the future. The
deed of those noble men and women who contributed to that
fund of idealism is as great as the one performed by the editorial
writer who restored the faith of a little child. These unidentified
men and women have restored ideals to seven youths of today
who will be men of tomorrow. They have proved to those boys
that principles do mean much and have saved for the future of a
nation and the salvation of democracy seven splendid citizens.
We pay them homage with this humble tribute in our own inade-
quate manner.[5]

It was a few years later when, as city editor of the *New Orleans
States*, Hebert broke the first story on the Louisiana Scandals
which led to an exposé of graft and corruption at the highest state
level. Among those implicated and later imprisoned was the president of Louisiana State University. Although a sad travesty, it

might be said justice for journalism was served when Hebert dispatched one of his reporters to cover the return of the handcuffed university president, and the reporter—by fate and city editor circumstance—turned out to be one of the seven students expelled from LSU.

As a newspaper reporter, Hebert's career ran the gamut—politics, hangings, hold-ups, sports, beauty contests, name bands of the 1930's and the great and to-be-great jazz musicians on his Bourbon Street beat, such as Al Hirt, Louis Armstrong, Papa Celestin, Pete Fountain, Louie Prima, Sharkey, and on down the list.

In January 1935, a deadly, dapper killer named Kenneth Neu was awaiting execution by the hangman's noose at Parish Prison in New Orleans. Cocky and confident he would be spared, Neu's bravado and ballad singing when others walked to the gallows was widely publicized. But when all appeals failed and his fate sealed, Kenneth Neu sang no more and barred the press. Hebert had covered Neu's capture and trial and his imprisonment on death row. In his column of January 16, 1935, Hebert wrote about Kenneth Neu:

> In less than a fortnight a man is going to be hanged by the neck until he is dead—dead—dead. Kenneth Neu, dapper killer of Sheffield Clark, will expiate his crime against society at the end of a rope in the Parish Prison. The fact that a man is going to be hanged is of no particular importance at the moment—hundreds of men have been hanged for the crime of murder in years gone by and hundreds of men will be hanged in the future. The thing that is important is how this man is going to die. Will he go to the gallows with the audacious bravado that has characterized him? Will he wilt under the strain of approaching death and die a cringing coward? Will he walk to the gallows with a song on his lips in the manner that he has bellowed popular ballads while fellow prisoners have been led to their doom or will he be carried to the trap by the strong arms of prison guards?
>
> I'll answer the question of how Kenneth Neu is going to die. I'll answer it with reservations but definiteness in conclusion. According to reports coming from the cell of the murderer, Kenneth Neu has sealed his lips against song and moves them only in

fervent prayer. Those who have seen him recently say that the calloused killer has become the penitent sinner awaiting inevitable death. In the accuracy of those reports lies the answer to the question of how Kenneth Neu is going to die. If he is sincere in his statement that he has repented and has embraced religion, he will die bravely. If he is sincere, he will walk to the gallows' trap, unaided and unafraid. If he is sincere, he will die buoyed up by the comfort of religion. If he is not sincere, he will be carried to the gallows—he will collapse. Kenneth Neu's only chance for a brave death is his heart—his only hope is religion.

I have never seen religion fail men on the gallows. I have seen murderers die—I have walked up the gallows' steps with men who have killed and I have heard their last words—I have spent the last night on earth with men who were to die in the morning—I have received the last message from men who were to be killed because they had killed. In each instance where there was a deep and sincere regard for religion, I have seen the condemned men walk unhesitatingly and steadily to their grave. Men may fail—hangmen may bungle their work—but religion never fails.[6]

Kenneth Neu read Hebert's column. On the day of his execution, fifteen minutes before he was to be hanged, Neu sent for Eddie Hebert. While the hangman stood by, awaiting his victim, Kenneth Neu stood tall and placed his hands on the prison bars. In a loud, clear, unwavering voice he sang his last ballad, *I'll Take You Home Again, Kathleen.*

In the sports arena Hebert covered such greats as Dempsey and Tunney at the old Louisiana Auditorium. But of all the greats of the boxing ring, it was a bantamweight bootblack from Houma, Louisiana, who was to make the greatest and most lasting impression on Eddie Hebert's life, for reasons both related and unrelated to boxing. His name was Pete Herman. One of his teachers in grade school had been a beautiful young schoolmistress named Lea Naquin who married Felix J. Hebert and became Eddie Hebert's mother.

Pete Herman became the bantamweight champion of the world and the first bantamweight to lose the world title and then regain it. In the late 1920's, during a fight with Joe Lynch, Lynch's glove lace came untied and whipped across both Herman's eyes. Pete Herman went blind.

In 1935, more than ten years before Eddie Hebert had any inkling of his own impending eye problems, he wrote a moving and deeply human column about the courage and fate of his friend, Pete Herman. It was prompted by a hastily scrawled postcard from Tennessee on which Pete Herman had written: "Hello, Ed, feeling fine, leaving in a few days . . . operation, I don't believe successful . . . Regards . . . Pete Herman. In his front page "Periscope" column of January 9, 1935, Hebert wrote:

> In that simple message on the back of a postcard from Memphis is the story of faith, courage, hope and undying spirit. The spirit of a mighty little man who wouldn't quit and who in the face of eternal darkness has the courage and the fortitude to write, "Feeling fine." For eight years Pete Herman, former bantamweight champion of the world, has been totally blind. Recently he took one chance in 10,000 and went to Memphis to have an eye specialist perform an operation on him in the hope of restoring sight. For eight years Pete Herman has hoped and prayed that his eye sight would be restored. For eight years Pete Herman has been led to his church to make repeated novenas. For eight years Pete Herman has lived in the hope that the eyes which brought him greatness in the prize ring would again flash with the brightness and accuracy that carried him to the height of his profession. He took the chance and he lost. The operation was unsuccessful. Unless a miracle is wrought Pete Herman will never, never see again. He is doomed to live the remainder of his life in darkness. He must continue to live under a light that has failed. His must be a world of sound but not of sight. Pete Herman knows all this; Pete Herman knows he is going to remain blind and yet he sends a card, "Feeling fine," supplemented by the simple notation, "Operation, I don't believe successful. . . ."

What a lesson most of us could take from the indomitable spirit of this fighting man. Even now he has refused to give up hope. "I don't believe successful," he says. In that simple statement he again throws out the challenge of hope in a hopeless world. Those of us who saw Pete Herman rise from bootblack to bantamweight champion of the world can appreciate the spirit of the man. I saw Pete Herman at the Louisiana Auditorium give Kid Williams a trouncing only to see the decision given against him for the championship. Undaunted, I saw him come back several months later and wrest the crown from the head of the little two-fisted Philadelphian. Later Pete Herman became the first champion to lose and win back his titular honors. Is it no wonder that Pete Herman refuses to quit now?

I have before me a tribute paid Pete Herman by Jimmy Wilde, the 'Mighty Atom' of Great Britain, whom Pete defeated before the Prince of Wales in London. It is a tribute from one great fighter to another. Herman won because he was the better boxer, Jimmy Wilde writes. 'He was the cleverest boxer I ever met. I rank him as the greatest bantam of my day. I do not know any 8st. 6lb. boxer who would have lived with him. Mr. Peggy Bettinson, who had seen all the world champions for half a century, said to me when I was dressed (after Herman had stopped me in the 17th round): "You have been beaten by the greatest bantam of all times. He knows as much about boxing as Jim Driscoll, Packey McFarland and Jim Corbett. It's no disgrace to be licked by such a perfect master. You are extraordinary, I must say, to have lasted 17 rounds with him." Poor Pete Herman! With all the sporting world at his feet he was, nevertheless, saddened by the verdict of a specialist that he was doomed to blindness. So, on the threshold of young manhood and world fame in sports, this quiet, swarthy son of Italy passed on to perpetual blindness.' Well said, Jimmy Wilde . . . a tribute well earned and nobly paid. You would be still prouder of Pete Herman if you knew him today. There perhaps would be a tear in your eye if you read the message which I received from him, but you would be proud of him because he hasn't quit yet. I wonder how many of us would pen the message of Pete Herman, "feeling fine" in the face of the same obstacles? I wonder how many of us would say we are feeling fine if we knew that we were faced with blindness for the remainder of our lives? I wonder how many of us would say we are feeling fine in the face of adversity or reverse. Surely we can all take a lesson from this gamester who is 'feeling fine'. Nightly, Pete Herman, with his brother, Gasper Gulotta, ever at

his side, sits in his Club Plantation in the Vieux Carre. Thousands
of guests come and go but he does not see one of them, though he
speaks to all. There is always a smile on his face—I have never
known him to complain. He is always 'feeling fine'. He has lost
the fortune which he earned with his fists in the ring. The wife he
loved has been buried in a grave Pete Herman has never seen. He
knows his children only by their voices and the touch of their
hands. Still Pete Herman refuses to lose faith—still Pete Herman
clings to a tiny ray of hope—still Pete Herman believes in his
God. Perhaps in another world Pete Herman will have the happiness he has sought in vain. Perhaps in another world Pete Herman will be champion again—that perhaps is why Pete Herman
today is 'feeling fine!!! . . .'" [7]

During the thirties Hebert, the reporter, was a familiar after
dark figure on Bourbon Street and in the plush gambling casinos
and supper clubs around New Orleans. He covered all the big
name bands at The Roosevelt, Club Forest and Suburban Gardens. He heard the music of those memory years played by such
names as Glenn Miller, Ted Weems, Guy Lombardo, Jan Garber,
Vincent Lopez.

He was always a judge at the big beauty contests. He was present and participated in the show business birth of such greats as
Dorothy Lamour, Dorothy Dell, and Mary Healy, all New Orleans born and reared.

Whether man shapes his destiny, or destiny the man, Eddie
Hebert's reporting became more and more the world of politics.

He had a front row center seat writing about Louisiana's rough
and tumble brand of politics and he wrote it as he saw it. He
claimed to be neither an accomplished writer nor a great writer.
That his writings demanded and captured attention was undis-
puted. Much like the artist who takes the blank canvas and uses
the broad or thin brush to express himself, Hebert used the stac-
cato beat of a reporter's typewriter to pound out thousands of
words on people, places and politics. His compositions were dramatic, flamboyant, with a tinge of the purple prose whenever pos-

sible. They were also hardhitting and probing, spiced with a quick wit and the catch phrase that often deflated the politician and delighted his readers.

Perhaps Hebert's political directions took a prophetic turn in 1930, under the Evangeline Oak in St. Martinville, Louisiana. It was there he covered Huey P. Long's opening campaign for a seat in the United States Senate. Hebert was to write dozens of stories about the Louisiana Kingfish, the political phenomenon from Winnfield, Louisiana, who parlayed a railroad commissioner's job into one of the most powerful political machines ever to emerge on the American scene.

In 1934, Hebert took time out to marry a Creole beauty named Gladys Bofill but quickly plunged back into reporting by taking advantage of a honeymoon in Havana as an opportunity to be one of the first American newspapermen on the scene when Fulgencio Batista came to power. He came away with exclusive interviews and photographs, not only of Batista, but with United States Ambassador Jefferson Caffery and President Mendieta of Cuba, as well. A few years later, Hebert's only child, a daughter, was born. She was named Dawn and Hebert steadfastly maintains the name was selected because of the time he customarily arrived home. (She is now married to John Malcolm Duhe, Jr., an attorney and a Republican, and with their four children live in New Iberia, Louisiana on the banks of Bayou Teche.)

On September 8, 1935, a nation was shocked when United States Senator Huey P. Long was the victim of an assassin's bullet, fired in the corridors of the State Capitol Building in Baton Rouge, Louisiana. Hebert was continuing to blaze newspaper trails and in 1937 was named city editor of the *New Orleans States*.

Two years later Hebert broke the first story of what was to become known as the Louisiana Scandals, an unfolding exposé of crooks, grafters and thieves who had inherited the political machine of the Kingfish and who had been keeping it well oiled at the taxpayers' expense.

The *States*, for the first time, was awarded the coveted "Sigma Delta Chi Award for Courage in Journalism," and Hebert was sought after throughout the country as a speaker on the Louisiana Scandals.

With the collapse of a once powerful and corrupt political structure in Louisiana, and with the 1940 elections approaching, change and reform was in the political wind. Eddie Hebert was thirty-eight years old. Looking back on Hebert's career at that point in time, he emerges as a newspaperman's newspaperman. His was the boundless energy that thrived in pursuit of a story; his was the zeal and unabashed professional pride to outwit his peers and come away with the "scoop"; his was also an appreciation of the freedom of the press and of the responsibility of the press. With a reporter's awareness, he developed tightly guarded contacts and lines of communication, protected his source, and from this forum reaped his rewards. His reputation as a reporter, columnist and formidable city editor was well established. The upward curve of his newspaper career showed no signs of dipping. Long after he stopped reporting the news and began making it, he continued to describe himself as a "reporter on sabbatical leave."

But in 1939, there was something else in the political winds of Louisiana. Fate and circumstances were slowly steering Eddie Hebert on a collision course with destiny, when he would relinquish one successful and legendary career to claim another.

With Louisiana still reeling from a jolting political hayride, Hebert made the decision to become a candidate for the United States House of Representatives from Louisiana's First Congressional District. When asked what motivated his decision, his breezy reply was that ten thousand dollars a year as a congressman beat $85 a week on the newspaper. He also explained that if elected he only planned to serve one term, as the privileges of an ex-congressman included lifetime access to the floor of the House of Representatives. Thus, he gleefully projected the exclusive coverage such access would mean to a reporter.

In the 1940 Congressional elections in Louisiana, Hebert defeated by a two to one majority Joachim Octave Fernandez, the incumbent who had represented the First Congressional District for ten years.

Hebert Goes to Congress

Hebert's life as a member of the Congress of the United States began at age forty.

On January 3, 1941, the reporter on sabbatical leave assumed officially the title of United States Representative from Louisiana's First Congressional District. At high noon on that day he raised his right hand and solemnly promised to defend and uphold the Constitution of the United States.

Later that month, Franklin Delano Roosevelt was inaugurated for his third term as President of the United States. Abroad, a former German paperhanger had goose stepped all over Europe, stamping the Nazi swastika from the Balkans to Scandinavia. A bombed and battered Great Britain still stood, infused with the sheer willpower of Winston Churchill. In June of that year Hitler's armies invaded Russia and in October the United States—not yet at war—began for the first time in its history a peacetime military draft.

On December 7, 1941, bomb-laden planes bearing the insignia of the rising sun streaked suddenly out of a peaceful Pacific sky; their target was Pearl Harbor. Eddie Hebert had been in Congress almost a year.

For the Louisiana representative, investigation was to be the name of the game and he approached his assignments with all the vigor and determination of a star reporter in hot pursuit of a front-page exclusive.

Hebert's first committee assignment was the District of Columbia Committee. One of his future committee colleagues was to be the freshman congressman from Massachusetts, John F. Kennedy.

Hebert promptly headed an investigation of the District's Police Department which resulted in the Department's complete reorganization. He also introduced legislation authorizing a Department of Corrections and sponsored another bill that established an alcoholic clinic for the District.

When election time rolled around in Louisiana, Hebert remained a reporter on sabbatical leave and was returned to Congress, again and again and again.

On Washington's Capitol Hill, Hebert gradually emerged as an investigator to be reckoned with. As a member of the old Naval Affairs Committee (later renamed the Armed Services Committee) he attracted nationwide attention during investigations of labor and financial disputes affecting production of planes under government contracts held by Brewster Aeronautical Corporation. The investigation resulted in the indictment and conviction for perjury of the labor leader at the Brewster plant who had given false testimony before Hebert's committee.

In 1945, Hebert was chosen a member of the Naval Affairs 5-man blue ribbon committee, headed by Congressman Lyndon B. Johnson of Texas, to officially tour post-war Europe, while the war with Japan still raged. Hebert and his colleagues were the first American civilians to enter Bremen, Germany after the war.

During this official fact finding tour, Hebert kept a diary in which he recorded his personal impressions and also the human reactions observed in the wake of war's end. His diary was later published and entitled *I Went, I Saw, I Heard*. On May 24, 1945, he made the following entry:

> The more I hear people express themselves the more firmly convinced I am that now is the time to 'talk turkey' with Josef Stalin and Russia. There's going to be trouble, and plenty of it, from Russia unless we deal firmly while our power is at its height. Power is the only language that Russia knows and respects. Reports now have it that Russia does not intend to release that section of Germany which is under its control, but will make it the 19th State of the Soviet Union.[8]

Back on the Washington scene, Hebert of Louisiana became widely known as one of the toughest interrogators ever to head a congressional committee. His deceptively innocent questions often packed enough verbal explosives to "blast" generals and admirals into orbit.

Hebert enjoyed and thrived upon the stir he created. In a *Saturday Evening Post* story, feature writer Jo Thompson described Hebert as "an egotist with strong and genuine prejudices, his terrific sense of humor saves him." [9]

But also a large measure of the man was the reputation he acquired for the fairness and impartiality of his committee hearings in pursuit of facts, and for his utter disregard for political party affiliation when justice was to be served.

In 1948, along with then Congressman Richard M. Nixon, Hebert served on the old House Un-American Activities Committee, at that time investigating the Hiss-Chambers case. In his book, *Six Crises*, Nixon wrote of Hebert:

> Hebert, a Democrat from Louisiana, was respected by both Republicans and Democrats in the Congress because, while he always fought hard for his party's position, he had made it known on several issues in the past that he was no rubber stamp for Democratic Administrations. [10]

From the other end of the spectrum, an observation by Whittaker Chambers in his book, *Witness*:

> For Congressman F. Edward Hebert (of Louisiana), the most unsparing of interrogators, I developed a respect based upon what I felt to be his firm grasp of the human factors in the Hiss Case, and his equally firm grasp of reality that made him at least extremely skeptical of the antics of Alger Hiss. [11]

Hebert appeared possessed of that rare knack for wresting the truth from a witness in a manner that commanded the respect and admiration of the witness. Neither did he ignore the effective use of dramatic impact in proving a point.

It was during his ten year tenure as chairman of the Armed Services Investigating Committee that he created his now famous "Chamber of Horrors." Under investigation was military waste through a hodgepodge program of purchasing at the taxpayer's expense. Hebert's committee was unable to obtain funds customary to such an investigation but remained undeterred in their objectives. With dramatic aplomb, Hebert set the stage for his investigation. The hearings opened with an odd assortment of tables and racks that looked like a bargain basement sale, displaying everything from light bulbs to tacks, complete with price tags, showing the wide range in cost to the government for identical items. Hapless Pentagon officials were seated in front of this "Chamber of Horrors" each day when called upon to answer questions of price disparity and the question of who was responsible for such slipshod military purchasing.

In his quest to nail down responsibility, Hebert caustically dubbed the elusive individual "The Phantom of the Pentagon."

"You know the Phantom," Hebert cracked, "he's the little man who's responsible for military purchases but he always seems to be gone. When I try to get him before the committee, he has just retired or left on a trip to the Far East." [12] He accused the Pentagon of hiring alibi artists and propagandists to confuse the issue and at one point was heard to demand the names and salaries of the "Potomac Pitchmen" writing the Pentagon's explanations.

Hebert's knack for catch phrases and his frequently biting sarcasm made his committee sessions hot news copy. He was a reporter's delight. He told it like it was in language anyone could understand. To a reporter's query, "Can I quote you?", a typical Hebert answer was, "I said it, didn't I?"

During Hebert's early years in Congress, few of the Pentagon powers could pronounce his name. They called him "Hee-bert" and had only vague recollections of the jovial fellow from New Orleans who had the swankiest office on Capitol Hill, complete with Southern hospitality and New Orleans cuisine. But before 1950 rolled around, everybody who was somebody at the Pentagon not only knew who he was but knew his name was pronounced "A-bear".

His investigations covered broad military areas; overcharges in defense contracts, the airplane industry, weapons systems management, alleged influence of retired officers of the Defense Department and alleged munitions lobbying affecting military decisions. His committee was acknowledged as one of the most effective and respected in Congress and was credited with saving the government billions of dollars. Although far down the ladder in committee seniority at the time, Hebert had been selected by Armed Services Committee Chairman Carl Vinson of Georgia to organize and head the powerful Investigating Subcommittee.

The congressional career of Eddie Hebert was now under full steam and surging onward. Some of his colleagues in the House such as Everett Dirksen, Richard M. Nixon and Lyndon B. Johnson, were making plans to run for the United States Senate. But the future of Eddie Hebert became locked in crisis. A cataract had been slowly growing, gradually reducing the vision in his right eye—his only eye with any vision. He felt those whom he represented in Congress should know of his eye problem and on July 8, 1947, in his weekly radio report from Washington, he told them this:

> Tonight in making this last report to you I approach the subject which I desire to discuss with a great deal of hesitancy and reluctance. I turned the matter over in my mind for a long period of time. And having examined it from every possible point in an effort to arrive at the correct and proper conclusion, I always arrive at the same answer.
>
> I arrived at the conclusion that you, the people of the First Congressional District who have sent me to Congress as your representative on four occasions by handsome majorities, must be taken into my confidence tonight if I am to keep faith with you. . . .
>
> Under no circumstances do I want you even for a moment to associate this revelation which I am going to make with a plea for sympathy on my part or a desire on my part to become a martyr. I believe it only just and fair that you should know the existing physical condition . . . which may affect the future health and future well-being of an individual who acts as your representative in the national Congress. I am only making a factual statement in as simple a factual manner as I know how and as I can. . . .
>
> I have become afflicted with a cataract. On my right and only good eye. This will make it necessary for me to undergo a serious and delicate operation.
>
> We try too often to keep secret the physical condition of our

public officials. I do not subscribe to the practice. . . . And you should be informed of the effect it will have on my future. Not on my future as an individual, but on my future as your representative. . . .

I hope you understand the picture I am trying to paint for you. I do not want you to get the impression that I have been incapacitated. I most definitely have not. I do not want you to get the impression that I have gone blind. I have not. And I do not want you to believe that I despair of the future. I do not. I just want you to know the facts. That is all.[13]

In 1970, 23 years after that broadcast, Hebert was still in Congress, serving his record shattering 29th year, at no time seriously challenged for reelection. In 1968 he received 86 percent of the vote. It was not until 1969 that he underwent eye surgery to remove the cataract.

Early in that year, Hebert was told by his friend and physician, Dr. George M. Haik, that he must undergo surgery to remove the cataract on his right eye. Time and sight had reached the moment of truth—and consequences—for Eddie Hebert.

With no sight in his left eye to fall back on, Hebert knew he faced the possibility of being left in total darkness. Always it had been his nature—in things of vital importance—to condition himself for the worst and to be prepared for that eventuality. This he did with his impending eye operation but he expressed one hope— that if not successful he would still be able to distinguish between the lightness of day and the darkness of night, and not be locked in eternal darkness.

Hebert's honesty and easy rapport with the news media in Washington and their esteem for him over the years, were perhaps never more poignantly expressed than in a broadcast by Washington newscaster Joseph McCaffrey, when Hebert's eye operation was announced. This is what he had to say:

Next month one of the most colorful men in the United States Congress, the big, witty F. Edward Hebert will enter a New Orleans hospital to undergo eye surgery. The warm-hearted, gregarious Hebert will be carrying with him the wishes and prayers of thousands of men and women from all walks of life, from generals to denizens of the famed Bourbon Street the Congressman knows so well.

The operation is more than a routine operation because it will be performed on the only eye the Congressman has. Because of this he put off for years the decision to have surgery to remove the cataract. He put it off until his vision was so impaired that it has now become difficult for the Congressman to function normally....

At the time the cataract was first discovered in 1947, Hebert publicly announced it and expressed the determination to carry on as long as possible. He has been under medical observation since that date, but in recent years his vision has deteriorated. . . . With special glasses, Hebert has conducted countless Congressional hearings, and a stranger would never know that he had a vision problem.

With Mr. Nixon in the White House, Hebert has a unique distinction. For the third time, a man with whom Hebert served in the House and on the same committee, occupies the White House. Overall, Mr. Nixon is the sixth president under whom the big, robust New Orleans Congressman has served.

It all started when Hebert served on the House District of Columbia Committee. John F. Kennedy, a youthful Representative from Massachusetts, was later to become a member of that committee. When Lyndon B. Johnson was a House Member from Texas he served with Hebert on the old Naval Affairs Committee, and later both were members of the Blue Ribbon Committee which toured Europe after World War II. During the famous Hiss-Chambers hearings Hebert was on the House Un-American Activities Committee with Richard Nixon.[14]

In early March of 1969, Hebert entered Hotel Dieu Hospital in New Orleans and a team of doctors headed by Dr. George M. Haik, removed the cataract.

There followed long, slow weeks of light and darkness and shadowy outlines. To a man of Hebert's temperament—not distinguished for his patience—the hoped for vision at the end of the road tempered his wait.

I stood by with Mrs. Hebert in anxious anticipation the day they put the first pair of "practice" glasses on the Congressman. He stood in the middle of the room and slowly moved his head from side to side, uttering not a sound. He suddenly stalked from the room with an entourage in anxious pursuit. We followed him from room to room. Perhaps for the first time in his life, the debater, orator, ad-libber and skilled extemporaneous speaker was at a loss for words. For the first time, he was seeing in detail the interior of his home with a clarity of color perception unknown to him for twenty years. He then went from person to person to see the details of faces—blurred and clouded to his vision for so many years. Indeed, it was an experience that challenged the adequacy of words to describe and express.

Still ahead were months of adjustments familiar to cataract patients. A year later, Hebert faced another crisis when he was threatened with a detached retina. Once more he won his fight for sight and with the damage repaired resumed his official duties, plunging once again into the familiar role of investigator as chairman of the special sub-committee appointed to investigate the My Lai incident.

Hebert's refusal to play the game of politics according to party affiliation incurred the displeasure of President Truman following the presidential election of 1948.

A staunch advocate of State's Rights and with deep rooted beliefs in the constitutional sovereignty of the States, Hebert declined to support the Democrat's standard bearer for the office of President in 1948. He took this position following the Democratic Convention in Philadelphia when a civil rights plank, whose target Hebert felt was the South, had been included in the Democratic platform. Hebert removed his name from the Truman-Barkley ticket. When Barkley brought his campaign to New Orleans, Hebert refused to appear on the platform with the candidate for Vice-President.

Following the Truman-Barkley victory, Hebert's name was quietly omitted from the Un-American Activities Committee when the new Congress convened, on the pretext that Hebert was not a lawyer. When questioned about it, Hebert remarked that they didn't "omit" him but that they had "kicked" him off because he ran on the States Rights ticket and that the "Trumanites" just didn't like his exercising political independence.

Although it was not evident in 1948, Hebert was to develop a great respect and admiration for Harry Truman. Today on the wall behind Hebert's desk in his District Office, only three pictures hang—President Truman, President Eisenhower, and Richard Nixon before he became President—all bearing warm, personal inscriptions.

Although bounced from the Un-American Activities Committee, Hebert retained his assignments on the Armed Services Committee where his responsibilities and power continued to grow. While his vision was limited, this fact was not evident to the casual observer. He continued his rapid, yard long strides down Capitol corridors and on occasion personally escorted constituents on House and Senate tours. The challenges and frustrations he encountered and overcame can only be imagined by others similarly afflicted. Eddie Hebert scorned self-pity and did not share his problems with others. When asked for a copy of a speech he had delivered, his typical, matter-of-fact response would be, "What would I do with a prepared speech since I couldn't read it?" More and more he was sought after as a speaker. His smooth delivery and extemporaneous oratory, spiced with a quick wit, were a welcomed change from the customarily written and read speeches.

As an interrogator of witnesses, Hebert's eye condition had its humorous side. He used a microscopic eyepiece over the right lens of his glasses when he had someone on the witness stand whose reactions and facial expressions he wished to observe more closely. While it was old hat to committee members, not so to witnesses— who would stare in disbelief when Hebert would dramatically pull out the large, black appurtenance and attach it to only one side of his eye glasses. Many witnesses, whose testimonies had unhappy endings, were firmly convinced Hebert had put the "evil eye" on them.

In May, 1951, Hebert was chosen an official observer of the H-bomb device test at Eniwetok in the Pacific. He wrote the only eye-witness description of the blast. He described the experience in a series of articles cleared for security by the Atomic Energy Commission for publication in the *New Orleans States*. Copyright privileges were released by the *States* on publication and the series carried on front pages of newspapers throughout the nation.

On June 15, 1951, U. S. Supreme Court Justice Robert H. Jackson wrote Hebert: "Your account of the Eniwetok atomic experiment is one of the most effective uses of the mother tongue that it has ever been my privilege to read. It made me feel that I was sitting beside you and I cannot refrain from expressing appreciation of your craftsmanship." [15]

The series was recommended for the Pulitzer Prize.

The Congressman and The Secretary of Defense

It can be said that Hebert's tenacity and no-holds-barred reputation established as a reporter and embellished as a congressional investigator, were never more in evidence than when Robert S. McNamara was Secretary of Defense.

Secretary McNamara was constantly under fire by Hebert's committee in broad areas of conflict between the Congress and the Pentagon. During his seven year tenure as Defense chief, it can be said that McNamara was unable to claim a single victory over Mr. Hebert of Louisiana.

When McNamara announced cutbacks in the B-52 long-range bombers and suggested use of the faster TFX fighter planes as the advanced bomber for the United States, Hebert challenged the military wisdom of McNamara's decision and scheduled committee hearings with the Secretary of Defense as the lead-off witness. "What Secretary McNamara doesn't say," announced Hebert, "is that in order for the TFX planes to go faster they must be refueled twice as many times in the air, and I am sure the enemy will accommodate us by allowing us the needed time to do this in midair." [16]

When McNamara attempted to merge the Reserve forces with

the National Guard, Hebert promptly announced there would be no merger. As Chairman of the Subcommittee on the Reserves, Hebert developed anti-merger legislation and rammed it through against all the Pentagon's verbal artillery. The bill, known as the Reserve Bill of Rights Act, established and guaranteed the autonomy and integrity of the Reserve organization and the National Guard to prohibit mergers.

When McNamara announced the abolishment of the Junior ROTC programs in high schools and requested Congress to cut back the Senior ROTC programs, Hebert again picked up McNamara's guantlet. He sponsored and pushed through the 1964 ROTC Revitalization Act, known as the Hebert Bill, which gave the ROTC programs a statutory basis throughout the country and increased the number of units to include Navy, Marine and Air Force, in addition to the Army. Of this legislation Hebert said: "If I should be asked what I would like most to be remembered for during my service in Congress, I would unhesitatingly say the role which I played in establishing the ROTC programs in this country."

About the only quality shared by Hebert and McNamara was a dogged determination, not so much stubbornness, as an unrelenting tenacity and singleness of purpose in pursuit of their objectives.

McNamara was often described as the personification of the computer systems upon which he relied for his long range planning. Hebert's opinion of the computer was at the other end of the pole and blazed openly when attempts were made to computerize human factors. He hammered away at McNamara's theories and his cost efficiency programs. He constantly warned that national security was being sacrificed to implement McNamara's insistence on cost effectiveness. Relentlessly, Hebert bucked the Secretary of Defense for more nuclear ships for the Navy and for an anti-ballistic missile system, warning that the real cost might be in human lives instead of dollars and cents.

In spite of Hebert's frequent disagreements and vocal controversies with McNamara, a mutual respect, born under unusual circumstances, existed between the two men. Although locked in violent disagreement at every turn, it was also apparent that each respected the other's right to disagree.

Hebert never doubted that McNamara's objectives were motivated by what McNamara felt was best for the country. Hebert simply felt that such objectives, if pursued, would be disastrous for the country and used every blocking technique to thwart the Secretary of Defense.

Hebert's growing concern for the future of the military and for the Vietnamese situation with McNamara calling the shots, became a constant clarion. He deplored the prolonging of the war in Vietnam through limited targets and ineffective bombings decreed by McNamara. He urged that the United States go all out to win in Vietnam or get out. When asked whether he was a dove or a hawk, Hebert's reply was, "I'm a hawk, but no dove ever wanted peace more than I do."

In appraising President Johnson's reelection prospects, before the President had announced he would not be a candidate, Hebert remarked that Johnson's biggest political liability was a "two-headed monster"—the Vietnam war and how it was being conducted and "the Secretary of Defense, a dove, in charge of the war." [17]

In November, 1967, when Secretary McNamara resigned, columnist Drew Pearson hinted that Hebert, "the resourceful and able member of the House Armed Services Committee," [18] had been instrumental in bringing about McNamara's demise from the top Defense post. In typical style, Hebert immediately issued a statement which coincidentally appeared in the *New Orleans States* on the same page as the Pearson column. Hebert said:

> It reads like one of Grimm's fairy tales. At no time have I ever plotted, connived, urged or solicited the aid of Drew Pearson or anybody else to get rid of Secretary McNamara. Had the thought ever entered my mind, I think the record of my performance as a congressman clearly indicates that my tactics to accomplish my goals or objectives have been tactics openly employed, forcefully pursued and publicly announced. I have never found it

necessary, during nearly 27 years in Congress, either to solicit or depend upon someone else to speak for me or to fight my battles.

My disagreements with Secretary McNamara on numerous occasions have been lively and publicly stated. Our areas of differences are well known. Nor is it any secret that I have always expressed admiration for his intellect and tenacity for doing what he thought was right and what I thought was wrong. However, I think the Secretary and I share a mutual respect for each other. This is all I ask of anyone with whom I disagree. How could I connive to get rid of Mr. McNamara when I will miss him so much? Where now will I go for excitement?[19]

Congressional Activities and Accomplishments

Hebert's reputation as a defender and champion of the man in uniform, his undiluted and uncompromising brand of patriotism —as intense today as when he penned his essay at Jesuit High back in 1918—plus his fearless and personal stand in defense of that which he believes to be right, have blended to produce a most unusual man.

As the second ranking member of the House Armed Services Committee, he wields broad power from a forum of considerable influence. He chairs Subcommittee No. 2 which has been called the "workhorse" of the full committee. He also chairs the subcommittees on Military Retirement, the Service Academies, the special oversight committee on the draft, in addition to serving on the Armed Services Policy Committee and the Central Intelligence Agency subcommittee. He was also selected during the First Session of the 91st Congress, to head the My Lai investigation for the House Armed Services Committee. In making the appointment, Chairman Mendel Rivers said Hebert was "the most experienced investigator on the entire Armed Services Committee and he will call a spade a spade and let the chips fall where they may." [20]

In the 91st Congress, Hebert was also appointed to serve on the House Committee on Standards of Official Conduct, more commonly known as the Ethics Committee.

As Chairman of the Service Academies Subcommittee, Hebert

has worked hard to unify the three major academies for the Army, Navy and Air Force and has given top priority to maintaining their uniformity. For a number of years he has been striving towards passage of a bill that would establish a Uniformed Services Military Medical Academy, or a "West Point for doctors," as he puts it. He has strong feelings about the need for such a facility and with the opening of the 91st Congress—and with a maximum of expert maneuvering—his bill received the coveted HR-1 tag, as the first bill to be introduced in the new session of Congress. His bill envisions a Medical Academy that would provide a complete medical education for the individual who, in return, would serve a prescribed number of years in the armed services. Hebert feels such an academy would assure the military of much needed doctors and would permit civilian doctors to remain in private practice where they are needed to serve local communities.

Hebert, still a sports lover, has also been a strong proponent for permitting the service academies to play in bowl games and received credit for the Naval Academy's acceptance to play in a New Orleans Sugar Bowl game. As a member of West Point's Board of Visitors, he introduced a motion to allow the Military Academy to accept bowl invitations, citing the precedent already set by Air Force and Naval academies' participation in bowl games. Hebert remains confident the Secretary of the Army will reconsider a previous decision and allow West Point to accept bowl invitations.

Because of Hebert's Armed Services Committee assignments, it follows that the bulk of legislation under his sponsorship has pertained to military and defense matters. However, he has also sponsored legislation of significant importance to his district area. Of particular notice was legislation he introduced to authorize construction of the Mississippi River-Gulf Outlet. This channel outlet reduced the distance from the Gulf of Mexico to New Orleans by about 50 miles, a tremendous time saving and economic boost for the Port of New Orleans.

Hebert also authored the first bill introduced to give Louisiana tideland rights and has continued his support of this long struggle.

It was through Hebert's efforts and sponsorship that Alvin Callender Field in Plaquemines Parish was established as a Reserve Training Center for all branches of service. It is the largest military installation brought to the New Orleans area since the Algiers Naval Station at the turn of the century. It is referred to as the Reserve Training Center that Congressman Hebert built and the Bachelor Officers' Quarters on the base is officially designated as Hebert Hall.

To insure that the Eighth Naval District would be permanently headquartered at New Orleans, Hebert sponsored legislation which accomplished this designation by law.[21]

Through the years, Hebert has also maintained a sharp lookout for surplus government properties that might benefit his district.

When surplus acreage was declared at the old Algiers Naval Station, he promptly took steps to make it available for non-profit hospital and/or educational facilities. Already underway there are projects expanding facilities of Delgado College and the Orleans Parish School Board. Hebert also arranged for a joint parish participation of surplus land at Jackson Barracks for educational and police training purposes.

When the five hundred acre site of the old Naval Ammunition Depot at Belle Chasse, Louisiana, was no longer needed for that purpose, Hebert put the wheels in motion to acquire the tract for Tulane University's use as a scientific laboratory research center.

Dr. Herbert Longenecker, President of Tulane University, had this to say about the Congressman:

> I've known Eddie as a Tulanian, as a public servant who ably represents his district, his state and his country, as a champion and sometimes a very severe critic of the Defense Department, and as a number one champion of the Reserve Officers and the Reserve Officers Training Program. In other words, an old-fashioned patriot, who has spent a great deal of his years in Congress working to preserve our military strength and our national freedom.
>
> I know Eddie Hebert also as a man of great intelligence, a man who is warm and blessed with a marvelous sense of humor. And,

as a man of great determination, willing and able to take on any adversary and to fight for what he believes to be right.

He has been active in the affairs of Tulane since his days on campus and his activities have in fact increased rather than diminished with the passing years. I believe Eddie's greatest contribution to Tulane . . . was his assistance in acquiring for the University the 500-acre site of the old Naval Ammunition Depot in Belle Chasse. This property has provided Tulane with an opportunity to greatly expand its scientific efforts . . . the scientists developed in these laboratories and the marvels they will produce, all will be tribute to the Congressman—for all will be products of the 'F. Edward Hebert Center of Tulane University.' [22]

A Second Legend and Recognitions

On January 3, 1966, at one minute past noon, the former city editor and reporter on "sabbatical leave" became the first individual in the history of the State of Louisiana to serve 25 consecutive years in the United States House of Representatives.

To commemorate the milestone, a life size portrait of the Gentleman from Louisiana was unveiled and hung in the Presbytere of the Louisiana State Museum in New Orleans; the first time in the history of the museum that the portrait of a living person had been placed on public display. Hebert had now become a second legend in his own lifetime.

The portrait had been commissioned by a group of civic and business leaders of the community and painted by John Clay Parker, a well-known New Orleans artist. Although the portrait's title will remain with the Hebert family, the work itself is on perpetual loan to the Louisiana State Museum.

The principal address at the unveiling ceremonies was delivered by Hugh M. Wilkinson, President of the Louisiana Historical Society. The address included the following remarks:

Today we are gathered in this building—itself a monument of Louisiana's fascinating colonial past—to mark a very important date in the career of a great Louisianian of the present era—one of the very greatest, I do not hesitate to affirm on this day and time; to furnish him, by our presence, a testimonial of respect, admiration, esteem, and even our deep affection; and to be witnesses to the unveiling and first public viewing of such a re-creation, full length, on a painter's easel, of his features and figure as we know them so well, a portrait from a master-artist's brush, and one upon which men, women and children, for generations and generations to come, may look, and be pridefully reminded that the subject of this portraiture is one of the truly great statesmen, not only of Louisiana, but of the entire constitutional republic of these United States of America . . . he solemnly swore to preserve, protect and defend the Constitution of the United States . . . no member of the federal government has kept that oath more sincerely, more conscientiously, more unselfishly, more honorably and with a greater degree of scrupulous fidelity, realistic understanding and effective ability in the discharge of his legislative duties than Eddie Hebert.

. . . to Hebert the virtue has always been in the struggle, not the prize. His accumulation of this world's goods is modest, because he has never sacrificed principle to selfish advantage. Politically, he has never worn any man's collar, nor even any faction's badge which he could not readily put aside when his country's best interest so required . . . .

I consider F. Edward Hebert the closest example of, and exponent of, real statesmanship and genuine patriotism whom the Congress of the United States has afforded in the last 25 years. In the hands of men such as he, we can rely that the Constitution and the nation always will be safe against communism and every other peril of this exceedingly perilous age.[23]

On April 27, 1966, a civic banquet was held at the Royal Orleans Hotel in New Orleans to honor Louisiana's distinguished congressman. Hebert made only one request—there would be no speeches. In lieu of speeches there was a documentary film of Hebert's life—spiked with hilarity and humor and based on known and little known facts—narrated by television newscaster Mel Leavitt. The only formal note of the evening was a presentation of a silver punch bowl bearing the following inscription:

May this gift well mark the day of April 27, 1966, when friends privileged to know greatness gathered to honor the 25 consecutive years of service in the halls of the Congress of the United States by a statesman who in historic years of war and crises transcended the limit imposed upon few men, rendered legendary service to the destiny of his country, distingiushed his native state before the nation and gave meaning to the name of Eddie Hebert beyond the power of words.

The Naval Air Station at Alvin Callender Field in Plaquemines Parish paid official tribute to the Congressman by designating the Bachelor Officers' Quarters "Hebert Hall" and the Plaquemines Parish officials dedicated a new thoroughfare as "F. Edward Hebert Boulevard." In nearby St. Bernard Parish, "Congressman Hebert Drive" was officially dedicated.

The Marine Corps Reserve Officers Association created a new chapter in the New Orleans area known as the "F. Edward Hebert Chapter."

During the 250th anniversary celebration of the founding of the City of New Orleans, Hebert was selected the outstanding political figure in the city by the Francis T. Nicholls High School.

It would be impossible for one person to paraphrase the impressions of others to the actions and deeds of Eddie Hebert during almost three decades in Congress. With this limitation in mind, I have selected the words of colleagues, friends and other forms of recognition that speak eloquently, honestly and humanly of how others have seen and continue to see the gentleman from Louisiana.

One of the most effective and respected members of Congress during his long tenure was Congressman Carl Vinson of Georgia. He was chairman of the old Naval Affairs Committee of the House and when this committee became the House Armed Services Committee, Vinson was its first chairman. A friendship born of mutual respect and admiration developed between Hebert and "Uncle" Carl that was to continue long after Chairman Vinson retired to his farm at Milledgeville, Georgia, still consulted on occasion as the elder statesman. In reminiscing about Hebert, "Uncle" Carl said:

> Eddie Hebert has done a magnificent job in Congress. He is one of the most able men I have seen come to Congress during the more than thirty years I have been here. As Chairman of the House Naval Affairs Committee I have always been able to depend on Ed Hebert for the best and finest in a Representative.[24]

Congressman L. Mendel Rivers of South Carolina who succeeded Vinson as Chairman of the House Armed Services Committee and who serves in that capacity today, describes Hebert in these warm and human words:

> Eddie Hebert is, without a doubt, the most unusual character I have ever known, and when I say character, I mean all the good that this word implies. We came to Congress together back in 1941, and from the day we took our respective oaths we have been fast friends. Fate put us on the same Naval committee together, the old Naval Affairs Committee, and thereafter we were both assigned to the now Armed Services Committee.
> Eddie Hebert is a man of most unusual accomplishments. He is one of the best informed men one could ever possibly meet. He works hard, he works tirelessly, and he gives the extra effort to perfect any legislation coming under his jurisdiction.
> I remember when I became chairman, I told Eddie—I said, 'Eddie, we got a rough job now, running this committee after Mr. Vinson is gone, and I've got to lean on you heavily—you have to be my right arm.' He didn't know that he was going to handle more legislation than any member of the Armed Services Committee in its history. Immediately I assigned him to handle all of the Reserve matters, and he has done a job against the most insurmountable odds. I say this because all of his accomplishments have been during the McNamara era, when very little cooperation has come from the Defense Department. It was a new day for our Reserve components, that is, the Guard and the other Reserve parts of our Military. Eddie hasn't stopped there. When we passed the Draft Act, Eddie was one of the important members of this subcommittee which handled this legislation, and today he is head of the subcommittee which is the watchdog over the Draft

law with all of its ramifications, a difficult law and a difficult job. Moreover, the Military Academies come under his jurisdiction. He works hard and he works long. Now, if you superimpose these things over the responsibilities of the CIA Committee, the Policy Committee which runs the Armed Services Committee, and also the efforts of the authorization legislation containing over $22 billion, which is handled by the full Committee, you get some kind of vague idea of what this man does for America.

I hope he never quits Congress! God knows, I hope he never quits while I'm here . . . or while I'm chairman.

Just the other day I assured Eddie that he will have my complete support and a blank check in his efforts, over 16 years I might say, of trying to establish a military medical academy—and this will solve many of the problems of the shortages of physicians and other doctors needed for the military, as well as nurses and whatever else may be assigned to this committee.

Then you wonder why I say therefore that this is an unusual man? Oh yes, he's unusual! He knows the art of legislating, he understands the need of compromise, he's a warm person, and more than all of this he's a loyal friend. Mendel Rivers may be Chairman of the Armed Services Committee, but whatever record he's compiled it would have never been possible were it not for that old Louisiana Frenchman, God bless him, known as Eddie Hebert . . . .[25]

Colonel "Red" Blaik, former West Point football coach, has been a friend of Hebert's for thirty years. Although the friendship began through fate and circumstance, it has outlived the early circumstance of meeting and Colonel Blaik recalled his friend in this manner:

You know, it isn't often in life that you have a friend for over thirty years—but I have been very fortunate in having Congressman Hebert as my friend for these many, many years. It started when I was a coach at West Point. At that time he was very helpful to the Military Academy and to me in seeing that we got the right type of boys at the Military Academy . . . . There is no one on the Hill who has done more for the Naval Academy, the Air Force Academy, and the Military Academy than the Congress-

man. It's wonderful . . . to go into his office and to be greeted by a
friend who doesn't want to talk to you about the big things of the
day, but just about the ordinary things of life . . . .[26]

Another colleague and long time friend of Hebert's, though not
always sharing the same opinions, is Speaker of the House
John W. McCormack of Massachusetts, who has served consecu-
tively in Congress since 1928. In describing Louisiana's Dean of
the House Delegation, Speaker McCormack had this to say:

> . . . one of the outstanding legislators in the halls of Congress and
> a great American, Congressman Ed Hebert . . . one of the most
> active, dedicated, courageous members that I have ever served
> with. He's been a bulwark of strength to our country in this try-
> ing period of the world's history. And I can assure you that Ed
> Hebert is a leader in the national defense of our country. On many
> occasions I have asked him for advice on serious and trying prob-
> lems that confronted me as Speaker of the national House of
> Representatives, and his advice has always been sound and logical,
> and advice which I accepted . . . His contributions are already an
> integral part of the legislative history of our country. . . .[27]

Former President Lyndon B. Johnson, who served with Hebert
on the old Naval Affairs Committee, said:

> Congressmen are not born. They are made by driving energy
> and hard work, personal ideals based upon the needs of the spirit;
> a spirit of tolerance which makes possible working with other
> men in getting the job done. These are the respects in which Eddie
> Hebert measures up to the highest standards.[28]

Senator Mike Mansfield, who served with Hebert in the House
of Representatives, remarked:

> Congressman Hebert of Louisiana is one of the outstanding mem-
> bers of the House of Representatives; an advocate of a strong
> Navy, a clean and strong District of Columbia Government, and
> an outstanding worker in Louisiana's behalf.[29]

Senator Karl Mundt, also a former House colleague, declared:

> We need more independent and courageous men like Ed Hebert

of Louisiana here in Congress, if radicals and racketeers are to be driven out of public office.[30]

Former Congressman W. Sterling Cole, a Republican from New York, who later became Director General of the International Atomic Energy Commission in Vienna, said of Hebert, "A genuine American—thoroughly honest and unusually able." [31]

Another Republican, former Congressman William E. Hess of Ohio, said, "Hebert is a real representative of the people he represents." [32]

Claire Booth Luce, who also served with Hebert in the House, said, "F. Edward Hebert is one of the ablest legislators that the deep South has produced, and a very charming gentleman!" [33]

A few months before his death, Senator Everett Dirksen of Illinois, reminisced at great length about his early and growing impressions of Hebert during their service in the House of Representatives.

I had been in Congress about eight years, and at that time there arrived from New Orleans, Louisiana, a great big, broad-shouldered, husky fellow by the name of Edward Hebert. . . .

Despite the fact that we sat on opposite sides of the aisle, he on the Democrat side and I on the Republican side, we quickly developed what I felt was a firm friendship and that has endured in all these days. After 16 years in the House, I moved over to the United States Senate, and Eddie Hebert remained in the House, and in so doing he advanced his seniority position and in due course became, really, one of the influential people in the House of Representatives, particularly where our national defense and security were involved.

The newspaper training and background that he had a long time ago stood him in good stead . . . .

He has had a deep impact on the direction in Congress of a good many matters. He has influenced national policy in the right direction, and I can only say that I highly esteem the work that he has done in the national interest. . . .[34]

Senator Margaret Chase Smith who also served with Hebert in the House of Representatives, said this:

The aggressive and penetrating interrogations of my colleague,
F. Edward Hebert, in the Naval Affairs Committee hearings,
represent his forceful effectiveness in Congress.[35]

The foregoing excerpts of impressions and observations are
presented as a view of Hebert through the eyes of his peers at the
Washington level.

This biography would be incomplete without notice of some
of the other forms of recognition given Hebert at the local and
national level from groups and individuals aware and appreciative of his efforts and contributions.

As the first civilian to receive Louisiana's Distinguished Service
Medal, Hebert was cited

> ... in recognition of his significant, unselfish and untiring interest
> in the Louisiana National Guard and in furthering the security
> and welfare of the State of Louisiana and the United States of
> America . . . his profound wisdom in securing the activation and
> construction of Alvin Callender Field as the first joint-usage Re-
> serve Air Force . . . his wise counsel and steadying influence and
> his intelligent and practical approach to military problems have
> fostered a genuinely harmonious relationship between the mili-
> tary elements located in the New Orleans area and the people of
> Louisiana and all members of the Louisiana National Guard are
> deeply grateful and appreciative of his efforts in their behalf.[36]

For distinguished service to the Navy and the Army, Hebert
has been cited by the Navy League of the United States and by the
United States Army Association. He is also a recipient of the
American Legion's George Washington Great American Award,
given

> for meritorious service in the cause of and unwavering devotion
> to the historic principle of American Constitutional Government
> as exemplified by George Washington. . . .[37]

The Good Citizenship Medal from the National Society of the
Sons of the American Revolution was awarded Hebert

> ... in recognition of the splendid service which he has rendered

to the nation through his long membership in the Congress, with fidelity always to those principles of true patriotism and adherence to constitutional democracy as the way was pointed out for posterity by the founding fathers during and after the American Revolution.[38]

In 1965 Hebert was named "Man of the Year" by the Arnold Air Society which represents the nation's Air Force ROTC schools. He was singled out "in recognition of his untiring efforts in the introduction of and passage of the Reserve Officers Training Corps Revitalization Act of 1964." [39]

Also during 1965, he was named to the Minuteman Hall of Fame by the Reserve Officers Association for ". . . his genius and leadership to the cause of national security in both war and peace, has given meaning, substance and effectiveness to the citizen-soldier tradition vital to the safety and welfare of the United States of America . . . ." [40]

In 1967 he was chosen by the Reserve Officers Association to receive their "Man of the Year" award, as the individual "who has contributed most to national security of the United States." [41]

From the Military Order of the World Wars, Hebert was cited for ". . . distinguished and brilliant service in spearheading Congressional investigation that blocked the merger and prevented the reduction of the Army Reserve components." [42]

The Louisiana Historical Society presented Hebert with an Honorary Life Membership, "in appreciation of his record of outstanding public service, including a constant interest in the advancement of historical study and the preservation of historic monuments." [43]

A past president of the Young Men's Business Club of New Orleans, Hebert holds one of the limited Honorary Life Memberships of the club, presented him as

> A member of the Young Men's Business Club of New Orleans for over twenty consecutive years . . . as a member of the Congress has always demonstrated a devotion to duty and a courage to fight for the high ideals and principles which this club stands for . . . has always placed the interest of his country and of his people

above partisanship and has rejected national or local politics when discharging the duties and responsibilities of his office. . . .[44]

From his college fraternity, Delta Sigma Phi, Hebert received its Distinguished Service Award, "In recognition of distinguished service both within the circle of our fraternity and in the world at large, and in recognition of high ideals translated into action which has brought happiness to his fellowman and honor to the Delta Sigma Phi Fraternity." [45]

Several years ago, Hebert was honored by the State of Louisiana, the City of New Orleans, St. Bernard Parish Police Jury and the Plaquemines Parish Commission Council

> . . . in recognition of more than two decades of distinguished and continuous service in the Congress of the United States and . . . in appreciation of a consistently brilliant and effective record of public service . . . of inestimable value to the progress, prosperity and wellbeing of the people of the First Congressional District. . . .[46]

In this biographical sketch of F. Edward Hebert, I have attempted to take the reader back to the year 1901, and from there to travel forward to 1970, spanning the early and current life of the Gentleman from Louisiana.

With words, I have attempted to depict the changing scenes upon the stage across which Eddie Hebert has moved during the past 68 years.

I have tried to portray the boy, the young man, the newspaper reporter-city editor and ultimately the statesman.

I have attempted to present the credentials of F. Edward Hebert and to trace two successful careers of a most remarkable individual.

In this book, Glenn Conrad probes and analyzes the writings and words of the man who in his own lifetime has twice become a legend.

History will record the final chapter on the life of the Gentleman from Louisiana.

April 1970
New Orleans   —Virginea R. Burguières

CHAPTER II

AMERICA AND AMERICANISM

On Patriotism

SOMEWHERE DEEP WITHIN the soul of F. Edward Hebert is a feeling for these United States, for the people who inhabit them, and for the principles which unite these people, that cannot be fully described in words. Like the love of a man for a woman, or of a child for a parent, this is an emotion, something felt, something automatically accepted, not rationalized or discussed as casually as one would discuss the weather or a football game. On occasion, Mr. Hebert has given vent to this feeling regarding America and, in doing so, has expressed a great portion of his personal creed.

On July 4, 1947, in a radio address to his constituents, he asked some basic questions for all Americans and submitted his answers. Quoting from an editorial, he said in part:

What is patriotism?

It is not nationalism because nationalism is a silly cock crowing on its own dunghill.

It is not partisanship because partisanship has no points to its compass.

It is not imperialism because imperialism is concerned with extending real estate holdings.

It is not jingoism because jingoism thumps its chest and proclaims itself the heavy-weight champion of the world.

Then, what is patriotism?

Patriotism is a passion for the moral well-being of the state.

The first mark of the true patriot is personal morality. In it there is nothing selfish, coarse or ambitious.

As citizens and adults we must remember that children are not born patriotic. Patriotism is an acquisition; something imparted by parents, teachers, governments and churches.

What is America?

America is an aristocracy, not of blue blood but of clean blood.

America is liberty within law, similar justice for rich and poor, tenacious courage, abounding hope, true fraternity, and decent racial pride.

America is a spirit, an idea, a way of life, a personality.

America is Lincoln, Jefferson, Washington, Hamilton, Webster, Lee, Grant, Whitman, Carver, Jane Addams, Marian Anderson, and Colin Kelly.

America is Plymouth Rock, Valley Forge, Gettysburg, the Argonne Forest, St. Michiel, Bataan, Corregidor, Tarawa Beach.

America is the tiny village of the plains.... the clustering green roofs of a little town in New England . . . the great city's rushing roar.

America is the Flag, not inscribed with bird or beast of prey, but with the stars that redeem the night from darkness and the beams of red light that beautify the morning.

America is the ordinary side-street man and woman in whom the foundations are not shaken.

America is the executive, the farmer, the worker, the soldier, the sailor, the pilot.

America is the first immigrant and the last refugee.

Yes, America is a spirit, an idea, a way of life, a state of mind, and above everything else, America is a faith.[1]

The great symbol of America is, of course, those Stars and Stripes that have flown over this land for nearly two hundred years. Like all men with an appreciation of America and Americanism, Hebert has displayed a deep reverence for the American flag—not that bit of cloth at the end of a flagpole, but for what the cloth symbolizes—what it means.

What DOES the flag mean?

It stands for the principles set forth in the Declaration of Independence; it stands for the Constitution, the Bill of Rights, the Gettysburg Address. It stands for all the principles embedded in the growth and history of this country. The flag represents, too, all the sacrifices offered in times gone by to make those principles good.

Sometimes those sacrifices were offered by men who were brave enough to stand before their fellow citizens and make unpopular statements.

The sacrifices were sometimes offered in battle, in the faith that there are values greater than one's own life.[2]

On Individualism

But what, one might ask, has caused America to be all these things? What is the foundation of the greatness of America? Hebert's answer is summed up in a single word—individualism. He is devoted to the belief that man can rise above any human circumstance, if he has but the will to do so. Just as the pioneers willed to push the frontier westward, so, Hebert believes, can present-day Americans alter their destiny. This belief has been expressed on several occasions.

We were born in an era of rugged individualism where our sole weapons were our brains and our hands. The extent to which we used them was limited only by our desire and ability.[3]

On another occasion Hebert said:

America became strong because individual men and individual women were willing to fight as individuals to make it strong. America can never maintain that strength if it becomes a regimented nation where all individualism will be submerged in a gulf of so-called liberalism which is in truth a snare and a delusion.[4]

And finally, in a campaign address during 1944, Hebert said:

The backbone of this nation has been private enterprise, individual initiative and ingenuity and my every vote in Congress will be to continue that system.[5]

Frequently during his career, Mr. Hebert has warned his listeners about those persons who would sing them the siren's song of something for nothing, thereby undermining the individualistic structure of American society. Even though he was a supporter of Franklin Roosevelt's war-time leadership, Mr. Hebert became alarmed by certain domestic policies of the Roosevelt Administration, particularly when these policies related to the subject of individualism. As early as July, 1943, after only two and one-half years in Congress, Hebert told the members of the New Orleans Young Men's Business Club:

> This country was founded on individual efforts—rugged individualism, if you please—and it is going to survive only if we are allowed to regulate our lives and not be told what time in the morning we have to get up, what time at night we have to go to bed, what we can eat, and what kind of clothes we can wear. . . .
>
> There is a tendency in this country . . . to compress America. They [high-ranking officials] start at the top and chop down the big man. They call him a capitalist. . . . They chop him off at the top and drag him down.
>
> Then, down at the bottom of society is the lackadaisical fellow. The bureaucrats would grab him and drag him upward.
>
> Then you have, between those two factors moving in two directions, what you and I are—the great middle class. This is how America is different from the other countries—it has a great middle class, the strength and sinew, the body and soul of America.
>
> But these so-called social reformers would mesh them [the classes] together to have one central body indistinguishable from either top or bottom, and I say to you: What is that, if it is not totalitarianism? What is it, if it is not the same thing they have in Russia, in Italy, and in Germany? . . . You cannot survive in America—America cannot survive if we destroy the classes.[6]

The consequences of the abandonment of individualism can be most serious. This was emphasized by Hebert when, commenting in 1949 on the effects of the Truman Administration's welfare program, he said:

> This country—indeed the world—is being swept by an epidemic of the 'gimmes.' Nearly everybody wants to be given something at the expense of somebody else. . . .

1934—Reporter Eddie Hebert and Col. Fulgencio Batista of Cuba in one of first interviews following Batista's overthrow of Cuban government.

1936—President Franklin D. Roosevelt (seated left) and Reporter Hebert (lighting cigar) at Antoine's in New Orleans.

1940—Hebert enroute to polls with mother and brother, Gordon—Hebert's first election.

1940—Casting ballot with wife, Gladys, in his first election for Congress.

1943—Congressman Hebert and industrialist Henry Kaiser.

1943—General Claire L. Chennault, leader of the Flying Tigers, and Hebert on Chennault's first return to America after outbreak of war.

*1945—Congress-
man Lyndon B.
Johnson and
Congressman
Hebert at U.S.
Military
Cemetery near
Port Lyautey
in Africa.*

*1946—General "Lightning" Joe Collins rides in triumphant post-World War II parade
in New Orleans with Congressman Hebert and Mayor Robert S. Maestri.*

1946—President Truman signs Congressman Hebert's bill setting up a clinic for alcoholics in Washington.

1947—War Secretary Robert P. Patterson greeted in New Orleans by Congressman Hebert. In center is General Jonathan B. Wainwright.

1947—Congressman Hebert in New Orleans with Secretary of Navy James V. Forrestal and Admiral Aaron S. "Tip" Merrill.

1947—Generalis-simo Chiang Kai-shek signs "short-snorter" for Congress-man Hebert in Nanking, China.

1950—Political figures visit New Orleans French Quarter. From left: Congressman Hebert, Congressman Henry Larcade, Judge Leander H. Perez and Congressman Sam Yorty, who became mayor of Los Angeles.

1951—Congressman Hebert and Major General Anthony C. McAuliffe, hero of Bastogne.

1951—Congressional observers and atomic authorities at Eniwetok Atoll for observation of atomic weapons tests. From left: Hebert, Gordon Dean, chairman, Atomic Energy Commission; Lt. Gen. Elwood R. Quesada, who commanded the tests; Sen. Henry M. Jackson (D-Wash.); Rep. Melvin Price (D-Ill.) and Rep. W. Sterling Cole (R-N.Y.)

1953—President Eisenhower enjoys a laugh with Rep. Sam Rayburn (D-Tex.) follow-ing signing of Tidelands Bill. At center are Hebert and Sen. Russell B. Long (D-La.)

1954—Rep. Hebert with Pope Pius XII, Castel Gandolfo, Italy.

1958—New Orleans trumpeter Al Hirt performs at the Capitol. He is flanked by Rep. Hebert and Sen. Russell B. Long (D-La.)

1961—President Kennedy and Rep. Hebert at the White House.

1966—Attending a banquet in New Orleans are (from left) Congressman Carl Albert (D-Okla.) House majority leader; Sen. Allen J. Ellender (D-La.), and Congressman Hebert.

1966—Prinicpals at dedication of Hebert Hall at Alvin Callender Field near New Orleans are (from left) Mrs. F. Edward Hebert, Rep. Hebert, Mrs. John Malcolm Duhe, Jr., their daughter, and Mr. Duhe.

1966—Rep. Hebert with former heavyweight champions Jack Dempsey (left) and Gene Tunney.

1967—Rep. Hebert with Madame Chiang Kai-shek on a visit to Washington.

1962—(From left) Rep. Carl Vinson (D-Ga.), Rep. Leslie C. Arends, (R-Ill.), John Glenn, first American astronaut to orbit the earth, and Rep. Hebert.

1969—Admiral Hyman G. Rickover, father of the atomic submarine, with Rep. Hebert and Col. Ralph J. Maglione, Jr., former commander of the Air Force Thunderbirds.

1969—Rep. Hebert greets Astronaut Mike Collins whom Hebert appointed to West Point in 1948.

1969—A non-partisan discussion (From left), Rep. Gerald R. Ford, (R-Mich.) House minority leader; Rep. John McCormack, (D-Mass.), Speaker of the House, Rep. Hebert, and Miss Mary Swann, Hebert's Administrative Assistant.

1969—Rep. Hebert with Secretary of Defense Melvin R. Laird.

1969—Gen. William C. Westmoreland, Army chief-of-staff, enjoys a laugh with Rep. Hebert.

1969—President Nixon gives Rep. Hebert the pen he used to sign a bill amending the Selective Service Act to provide for a draft lottery. Rep. Hebert steered the bill to passage in the House. Looking on is Rep. L. Mendel Rivers, (D-S.C.), chairman of the House Armed Services Committee.

The more the government provides, the more is expected of
it. . . . [and]
One of the penalties of government assistance is a general low-
ering of the sense of responsibility.[7]

Then, in March, 1950, Hebert launched a verbal attack at those
persons associated with the Fair Deal who were willing to compromise American individualism. He said:

> The present generation was born into an era which first planted
> the seed in the minds of men that the government owed to each
> individual a living regardless of the effort put out by the individ-
> ual or the individual contribution made. In early life the seed of
> dependency was planted and the thought inculcated that every-
> thing will be taken care of by somebody else.
>
> It is little wonder today that the uppermost question in the
> mind of individuals is: How much am I going to get for nothing?
> How can I get a house without paying for it? What do I have to
> do to get a handout from the government without working for
> it? How can I get food, clothing and shelter without paying full
> value for them?
>
> That's the frame of mind of many individuals today.
>
> That couldn't just happen. That idea was planted there by
> demagogues, the medical quacks of public life, who, in order to
> get elected to public office and to gain temporary power, make
> outlandish promises which can only be fulfilled by spending the
> other fellow's money.[8]

Closely associated with Hebert's devotion to individualism is a
firm belief in the economic system that is best suited to support
political individualism. That system, of course, is free enterprise.

On Capitalism

> If you are familiar with my record in Congress, you will know
> that I am very much opposed to the Federal Government being in
> competition with private enterprise, and I have always voted
> accordingly.[9]

Hebert's views regarding capitalism and socialism have always
been to the point. A long time ago he took his stand as a champion

of free enterprise because he recognizes in that economic system one of the great foundations of freedom in America. During a campaign address in 1944, he emphasized the point that

> The backbone of this nation has been private enterprise. . . . Don't forget that it was private enterprise which furnished the manpower and the plants which made, in truth, America the arsenal of democracy. I am against taxation which will destroy private enterprise and private industry and which will make it impossible for private business and private industry to continue to exist.[10]

In his castigation of socialism, Hebert has never minced words, nor has he failed to draw the attention of his listeners to those individuals in government who, for their own reasons, toy with socialistic ideas. In 1951 Hebert told his constituents that

> Socialism is the great delusion of our times. It is perilous because it appeals to the weakness of man and places in the hand of the demogogic politican a weapon of appeal against which there is no defense because of the frailty of human nature. The appeal of this type of government is directed at the weakness to be found in most of us, a weakness which urges us to get along with the least amount of effort and to get all we can without putting out anything in return.[11]

The delusion of socialism is like an opiate that creates a dream-like sequence but once the drug's effects diminish, reality is hard to face. In this context, Hebert has said:

> I have never believed in a controlled economy because such regimentation is only an opiate which causes a terrific hangover the morning after.[12]

Indeed, Hebert completely fails to understand the rationale of socialism and socialistic schemes. He has said:

> It is a strange thing that we could ever imagine government control being for our benefit, when by no stretch of the imagination can a government conceivably be as interested in the people as the people are interested in themselves.[13]

In early 1949, after hearing President Truman's State of the Union message, Mr. Hebert became more specific about those who would toy with socialistic concepts. These remarks also marked the beginning of his uncompromising attack upon various proposals of the Truman Administration. Shortly after Congress met in January, 1949, Mr. Hebert observed that

> The Eighty-first Congress has every indication of being one of the most important, if not the most important, Congress in which I have served. I do not even except the war congresses. In those congresses the challenge to the American system came from beyond the shores of the United States. Today the challenge to our accepted American system comes from within our own boundaries and is suggested by no less a person than the President of the United States himself. . . .
>
> Whether we like it or not President Truman's message on the State of the Union was an arrow pointing in the direction of state socialism and collectivism and away from the road on which this nation has marched through the years of its unheard of prosperity and attainment.[14]

The following year the Congressman spoke of some of the consequences of socialism. He said that

> When one conscripts the fruits of one segment of society for the benefit of another segment and attempts to place all and everybody on the same level regardless of individual ability or capacity, one has started on the road to destruction of representative government and a democracy as we know it. That's socialism whether one wants to call it by that name or not.[15]

A short time later Congressman Hebert, criticizing the direction of the Truman Administration's domestic policies, told his radio audience that

> Socialism, statism, New Dealism, Fair Dealism, why quibble over words or phrases? Those who espouse them all walk the same road, they walk the road which leads to the ultimate destruction of a free and open system of government.[16]

On Freedom

In addition to defending political and economic individualism, Hebert has consistently gone out of his way to remind his constituents that it is up to them to defend their basic freedoms. Indeed, about commencement time each year, Hebert has offered a simple piece of advice to the young people of America: "Don't sign over your freedoms and rights for a lot of promises."[17] Long before the most recent fad among politicians to rise to the defense of the individual's basic freedoms and the rights of minorities, Hebert was acting. Due to his firm belief in the Constitution and what it stands for, Mr. Hebert has always acted to preserve the freedoms and liberties guaranteed in that document. He has always believed that the struggle for freedom is instinctive in most men, but, unfortunately, there is a struggle to control men which is seemingly instinctive in other men. Thus, he interprets the inner struggle as the age-old conflict between good and evil. He has persistently warned that

> People who love freedom must always retain control over their government; they can never let the government gain control over them. . . .[18]

So convinced is Hebert concerning the inherent right of liberty that he has frequently reminded his constituents:

> The Constitution does not give us liberty, the Constitution guarantees us liberty—that which we already have from the Creator.[19]

Long before the permissive era of the 1960's the Congressman recognized and identified the most serious evil confronting the liberty of the individual. In 1948 he said:

> Let us not bury our heads in the sand with the false security of the ostrich. Let us realize that freedom can destroy freedom, if not diligently, constantly, and intelligently protected and preserved.[20]

Twenty years later he succinctly stated the case for the American people:

This country can remain free only so long as Americans remain patriots.[21]

Throughout his life, but especially in adulthood, Mr. Hebert has been acutely conscious of the responsibility of older Americans to preserve in tact for present and future generations those freedoms that have been handed down from father to son since 1776. He is also aware of the fact that it is the duty of the present generation to know, understand and appreciate the basic freedoms enjoyed by Americans. Hence, Hebert has always welcomed an opportunity to address the young people of our country on the subject of patriotic duties. To a gathering of the student body of S. J. Peters High School in New Orleans, he said:

> Freedom is a wonderful thing, but it is not missed until you lose it. And if you in your tender years can only understand and appreciate what this great thing of freedom is, then you will have discharged your responsibility to the government and the nation that provided a constitution under which you live.
>
> Americans are free and will remain free only so long as they cherish that freedom.[22]

Similarly, Mr. Hebert has not hesitated to lecture his colleagues concerning their responsibilities to preserve the liberties of the American citizen of today and tomorrow. During one of the annual memorial exercises in the House of Representatives, he told his fellow Members:

> Ours is the task . . . to leave for future generations of young men and women an example of vision that is clear, unwavering and unfaltering. To do that, we, ourselves, must beware of the rocks which flank both sides of that hallowed shrine of liberty.
>
> On one side there is the dangerous rock of Scylla. It has often been camouflaged as Liberty, but we must know that is a liberty of indifference—indifference to truth, indifference to morality, indifference to justice, and more than all else, indifference to the social good. It is an alleged vaunted right of the individual to say, to do, or to think anything whatsoever he pleases—no matter who or what might suffer. It is based on the assumption that there is no absolute standard of right and wrong; it sets up the individual

as the supreme authority; it regards all regulation of liberty as unwarranted and unjustifiable restraint.[23]

Despite the fact that Mr. Hebert has been most explicit in his devotion to the Charter of this nation and to the basic freedoms which it guarantees to every citizen, there are people who, for reasons of their own—reasons riddled with selfishness—question, in the light of all his pronouncements on the subject, Mr. Hebert's sincerity and dedication to our instrument of freedom. On one occasion, the Congressman was treacherously misquoted after a meeting of the Armed Services Committee. A statement made by Hebert during the course of the meeting was sufficiently warped by some reporters to make it appear that the Congressman was opposed to the First Amendment to the Constitution. Hebert's response was instantaneous. After demonstrating from the record that he had been deliberately misquoted, Hebert said:

> I am a firm believer in the First Amendment—in the right of expression and the right of freedom of speech. The only thing I do suggest is that with each dissent or each expression of dissent must be carried a responsibility.[24]

It was either misunderstanding or the lack of a sense of fair play that produced the unbelievable misquote. Thus, Hebert was as concerned about the lack of a sense of fair play on the part of the person reporting his statement as he was about any personal implication that could arise from the whole affair. Indeed, a cursory survey of the record will readily indicate that Hebert conceives of fair play as being a hallmark of our democratic society. He has said:

> I have never attempted to be everything to everybody during my long tenure of office. The right of disagreement is fundamental in the concept of freedom as Americans understand it. I respect the right of any individual to express himself and to conduct himself according to the dictates of his own conscience. All I ask in return is respect for my own integrity and the right to discharge the duty and responsibility of my office as I appreciate it.[25]

Shortly after the episode arising from the meeting of the Armed Services Committee, Mr. Hebert restated his position in language that even his most ardent critics could understand. He said:

> I am a firm constitutionalist. I believe strongly, firmly and with feeling in the full expression of the Constitution of the United States as it was written.[26]

Amen.

On Americanism and Race

There are, unfortunately, many an uninformed person in regions of this country that would automatically conclude that F. Edward Hebert of New Orleans, Louisiana, is a typical Southern congressman (whatever a typical Southern congressman is supposed to be) when it comes to the subject of Negro Americans. These ill-informed persons would then drag out the usual litany of tired, overused and little understood words that supposedly describe the Southern congressman's attitude toward the so-called "Negro question" or "minority question." Hebert needs no apologist for his position with regard to any racial issue. Since entering Congress, his position has always been clear and consistent. He told a radio audience in March, 1949:

> I have always maintained that the Negro should have equal opportunities for education, advancement and development. They should have the opportunities to be trained in medicine, the law, and the other professions.[27]

A short time later, while many of his colleagues were developing the "race issue" for election purposes, Hebert verbally etched his position as a defender of equal opportunity for all Americans. He said:

> In the matter of race relations I believe in equal opportunity for every man to earn a living regardless of race, color, or creed. I do not believe that opportunity should be measured by a man's religion or a man's color. I do not believe that equal opportunity can be accomplished by force legislation which engenders hate and prejudice and deters attainment of the expressed goal.[28]

After World War II, Mr. Hebert began to discern that the tired and tattered football of racism was about to be kicked about again. He knew too that in the past the race issue had entered politics not because of any desire to improve the status of minority groups but in order that someone could win an election. Thus, in the late 1940's, Hebert noted that some of his colleagues in Congress were playing the very dangerous game of seeking votes by wringing the emotion of the race issue. He told his fellow New Orleanians:

> A great many people who wave the flag and pretend that they want to help the Negro are solely interested in perpetuating themselves in fat, lush jobs.
>
> A great many individuals who pretend to be working for the advancement of the Negro are seeking to use him as a pawn to be placed in the possession of any faction which appears at the time to best suit the purpose of these so-called leaders.[29]

Mr. Hebert's criticism of those who would use the race issue as a vehicle to secure votes has always been most vigorous. He has repeatedly accused these politicians of playing upon the very themes for which they accuse others of wrongfully adopting. In this vein he said:

> Of course, any observer of political patterns . . . knows that the aim of some political groups and political aspirants in announcing . . . a civil rights program . . . is especially calculated to attract racial and religious minority voting groups, particularly in the North and in the East. They pitch their campaign on a note of prejudice and hate, and sectionalism, the very things which they supposedly condemn.[30]

While many of his congressional colleagues were warming up their vocal cords on the Truman-sponsored civil rights program of the late 1940's and early 1950's, Mr. Hebert calmly restated his beliefs. His statement was not made in the House of Representatives, far from the scrutiny of his constituents, but rather he aired his views during the congressional campaign of 1950.

I believe and have repeated time and again that I believe every man, regardless of race, color or creed, should have relative equal educational and recreational opportunities to allow them the pursuit of happiness which is guaranteed by the Constitution of the United States.[31]

The 1950's are well remembered by many Americans as the McCarthy era, but the Army-McCarthy dispute was not the only issue claiming the attention of millions of Americans. The race issue was still very much alive and getting more lively as certain propagandists continued to shout embellishments of the facts. It was said that Southern politicians would do almost anything to "keep the Negro in his place." At the same time Hebert was saying:

> In America race, creed, or color should not be criteria by which our judgment of our neighbors should be based. . . .
> I have friends among the Negroes who suffer every day because of the color of their skin, and my sympathy goes out to them, but they should understand that the abolishment of segregation by law or regulation is not the answer to their problem. Education and understanding is the answer.[32]

This call for education and understanding as the key to the race issue was not simply a convenient catch-phrase for the moment. Within a short time after giving this advice, Hebert re-enforced his statement on the need for education to solve racial problems. He said:

> A nation has no resource more valuable than the education of its people.
> That is especially true of this nation, for our form of government is based on the beliefs of a free and informed electorate. . . .
> In turbulent times like these, the education of our citizenry is perhaps our greatest long-term strength.
> But today, that very strength is in peril. Our educational system is on the threshhold of a real crisis.[33]

The crisis, said the Congressman, was a crisis of shortages in facilities, personnel, and money. One can but speculate now whether the violence and disturbances of the 1960's would have occurred if more politicians of the 1950's had been willing to recognize the real solution to the race problem. They did not, apparently, note the need for improved education, the need for fact rather than emotion, or the need for planning rather than political rhetoric. Thus the racial troubles of the 1960's descended like a holocaust upon the country. As emotions born of the race issue rose to fever pitch, Hebert told his colleagues in the House of Representatives:

> I detest hate, racism, and bigotry. I come from Louisiana, the Deep South, and I am proud of the fact. I believe that every man has the right, regardless of race, color, or creed, to have equal opportunity. I believe in privileges for none, whether they be white, black, green, pink, or yellow.[34]

Six months later the Congressman told his constituents:

> Now, let's understand this clearly. I believe that every individual in this country . . . regardless of race, color, or creed should have the equal opportunity to earn a living. . . . I firmly believe that everybody in the country regardless of race, color, or creed should be equally represented and equally given the justice that is to be handed out by the courts, regardless of race, color, or creed. Now, I hope I make that clear. I cannot make it any clearer. I do not believe that everybody is created equal in the sense that each is given equal talent. . . .
> There is no racism in my veins—nor is there prejudice. I believe in each man standing on his own two feet.[35]

Returning to the youth of this land, in whom he has placed a great confidence for the future of America, Congressman Hebert expressed to the young people of Nicholls High School his views concerning Americanism and equal opportunity. During that address he said:

> Every American, regardless of race, color, or creed deserves an equal opportunity under law; but no American, regardless of race, color, or creed, should enjoy a privilege.[36]

This statement, too, is beyond further interpretation.

On the Draft, Dissent, Demonstrations and Destruction

Certainly one of the great issues of our time has been the war in Vietnam with all of the ramifications attendant upon that conflict. Mr. Hebert's thoughts regarding war in general and the Korean and Vietnamese wars in particular are presented elsewhere in this work. Here, however, an attempt will be made to focus attention upon some of the by-products of the Vietnamese war, especially those of a domestic nature, in order to determine the Congressman's response to some of these problems troubling Americans in the quarter century following World War II.

Very early in his career, Mr. Hebert expressed a concerned awareness of the necessity for a modern nation to be prepared for any eventuality that might result in war. Speaking in the closing days of World War II, he said:

> I believe that universal military training in peace time is the insurance of a nation against the pitfalls and unpredictable assaults against its way of life in the future. . . .
>
> Universal military service will not prevent war. . . . Universal military service and preparedness will put off the day of war and delay it and when war does come the nation best prepared and best able to defend itself and its honor and its way of life, will have the advantage of ultimate success at the cheapest possible cost in life and economy.[37]

At the same time, however, the Congressman was not blind to the thinking of so many Americans who view with dread the hardships and uncertainties of compulsory military service. To them he said:

> Any compulsory military service is hard, especially in a democracy like America. But remember, war is tough and hard and brutal.[38]

Preparedness, then, was forever on the Congressman's mind. Over four months before the outbreak of the Korean conflict, Mr. Hebert emphasized the need for preparedness when he told a radio audience:

I oppose the drafting of eighteen year olds for combat, but I favor the calling up of eighteen year olds for training.[39]

To underscore the necessity for adequate military training, Mr. Hebert came squarely to the point with regard to a long-standing problem for Americans. He said:

America has fought all of its wars with untrained or half-trained soldiers. And in every war thousands of these young men have needlessly died because they could not be taught to live. . . .

Politicians have condemned thousands of young men to death on the battlefield because compulsory peacetime training was politically inexpedient.[40]

Several months after the outbreak of the Korean conflict, Mr. Hebert restated his views concerning proper training for America's young men, and, at the same time, called upon his audience not to cast their eyes longingly in the direction of a by-gone era. He said:

The entire concept of American defense has been a small standing army in peacetime. Not being an aggressor nation, there is no need of a huge standing army during times of international peace. Because of the threat of aggressor nations to the peace of the world it has become imperative in times of peace to bolster the strength of our armed forces . . . .

Nobody in this generation who experienced the easy going days prior to World War II will ever live to see a return of those times and conditions. We may as well face the facts. We may as well realize and know that every physically able-bodied man who reaches the age of nineteen will have to give . . . military service to his country before he can plan on anything else.[41]

Just as the Congressman could understand the need for military preparation, so could he also understand and appreciate the human element of the individual caught up in the great machine that is universal training. He expressed his compassion when he said:

The young men of this country are not just pasteboard cards to be picked up and scattered around at home and abroad as the military brass desires. They are individual human beings, each with hopes and ambitions of his own; young men who will eventually be the leaders of this country.[42]

Coupled with Mr. Hebert's conclusion that universal military training is a necessity is his insistence upon better pay for servicemen. As long ago as 1949 he argued in favor of better pay for American soldiers, something that only became popular with the national administration some twenty years later. During a speech on national security, Mr. Hebert said:

> [Underpaid servicemen] . . . must lead to one inevitable result— poor guidance and direction of our national security and inadequate concern and instruction for the younger men in our military services.[43]

During the years following the Korean conflict and throughout the massive American involvement in the Vietnamese war, Mr. Hebert's regard for the necessity of preparedness remained firm. Then, as the struggle in Vietnam seemed to founder in the late 1960's, there were suggestions from some quarters that America might be better off with a volunteer army. Shades of 1776! Who isn't in favor of a volunteer army?—if it is possible—if it is realistic. As long ago as July, 1946, the Congressman expressed the desire that a volunteer army would suffice for the defense of the country.[44]

Two years later, as the Iron Curtain was ringing down on Eastern Europe and the Berlin Blockade was being effected by the Russians, Mr. Hebert had some reservations about a volunteer army. He said:

> I subscribe to the theory of volunteers if it will do the job, but if volunteers will not do the job, then I am in favor of the draft.
> We are all agreed that a volunteer army is far preferable to a conscript army, especially in time of . . . world peace.[45]

But it was not a very peaceful time then, and it has not been an especially peaceful world since 1945. Thus, when Mr. Hebert discussed the idea of a volunteer army in February, 1969, his thoughts were probably in reaction to the violence that was to be found around the globe. Obviously abandoning the cherished hope of a volunteer army in the near future, Mr. Hebert told a television audience:

> Before the present draft law was enacted into law, a year and a half ago, the matter of the so-called volunteer army was gone into in depth. . . . After all this debate, it was decided that a volunteer army was not possible or practical. Why not? The very fact that you have a draft law indicates you cannot have a volunteer army. If you had a volunteer army, you would not need the draft law.
>
> There is no place for a volunteer army, and I can say dogmatically to you that I believe there will be no volunteer army, regardless of whoever says there should be or should not be one.[46]

This view of the volunteer army was not born of the stalemate in Vietnam. The explosiveness of the international situation had prompted the Congressman to say during the course of an interview, when asked if the draft would soon end:

> No, . . . The draft is here with us to stay. We may not draft as many people. I think it very unfortunate that any suggestion was made during the political campaign [Presidential campaign of 1964] that the draft should be eliminated. It'll never be eliminated.[47]

Thus, Hebert's stand on selective service and universal military training is well known to those persons who know the man. What prompts such a stand? Is it too old fashioned to say love of country and the Congressman's desire to see national security maintained at the highest possible level?

The draft, the war in Vietnam, poverty, ignorance (on the part of both educated and uneducated people) produced, during the 1960's, an explosive situation throughout the country that had not been seen since the reckless, headlong plunge into the Civil War. Dissent, real or apparent, made itself the subject of most evening newscasts during the late 1960's. This was not especially unusual, for dissent in America is frequently equated with the proverbial apple pie. Hebert recognizes the right of dissent. He has said:

> The right to differ within the framework of the law is as Ameri-

can as the soil on which we walk and the flag under which we live. The application of that principle is entitled to a full Constitutional protection and must be respected in every forum, be it legislative, executive or judicial.

The American right to differ is expressed and protected in the principle that a person because of diversity of view, or misfortune, ought not to be intimidated, defamed, or degraded in a public forum against his will. So, the whole of it, in my very simple view, gets down to a question of the right of the public to know, but to the duty of the public to protect all of its citizens, great and small, uniformly and effectively.[48]

As the chorus of dissent in America rose, and sides for and against protest were clearly being formed, Hebert reminded his constituents of a most essential factor associated with dissent. He said:

Now I'll never disagree with anybody on their right to dissent. I'm a firm believer in the First Amendment and the right of expression, and the right of freedom of choice, but I certainly do suggest that with each dissent or expression of dissent must be carried a responsibility.[49]

Responsibility has always been a key word in the thought and actions of F. Edward Hebert. Frequently he has built what he had to say to his audience around that one word. Thus, in those days of confusion, dissension and worse, Hebert diagnosed what was perhaps the very root of the problem. He said:

The one great problem I think confronting this country, though there are many, but the greatest problem I believe is the lack of understanding in education on the part of the young people of this nation as to their responsibility to their country and as to what their country means and what organized society means. [Who is to blame for this situation?] I don't know. I do know this—that at a tender age, in the formative years of a young man's or girl's life the first principle they must understand is that they owe responsibility to their fellow man.[50]

Some persons have pointed out that the lack of responsibility among the youth of America is due primarily to something called the "generation gap." This might be simply an easy way out—an easy way for explaining away the responsibility of the parents, teachers and other adults to inculcate in the young a sense of responsibility. Hebert, along with many other thoughtful people in this country, is aware of the responsibility of parents to children and children to society. He has said:

> It is our duty, those of us who were born in another era, to give this generation the benefit of our own experiences, accomplishments and attainments under a system which allows us the freedom to do as we please and to make of ourselves the kind of men and women we desire to be.[51]

But in the uproarious days of the late 1960's there were many of the nation's young people, along with many who were not so young, who tended to disregard the formula of dissent plus responsibility. This led Hebert to remark:

> I am not concerned or moved to apprehension about what our fighting forces are doing in a war [Vietnam] which is not popular, and which we all admit is not popular. I'm not concerned with the ability of our fighting men in Vietnam. I'm not concerned with the military structure there because I know that victory will ultimately be ours. . . . But what does concern me, and causes me more apprehension, is what is going on in this country today. . . . Irresponsible dissension is more damaging to our cause of victory in Vietnam than any effort on the part of the enemy.[52]

The result of this situation described by the Congressman was predictable and the progression of the unhappy attitude was a certainty. From dissent with irresponsibility to demonstrations to riots with burning and pillaging, the progression was seemingly inevitable. In this regard, Hebert said:

> Can anybody be no naive as to think that the people who are allowed to lie in the street and block traffic, allowed to sit-in at people's places of business, allowed to interrupt military trains, are not going to go further, and further and further.[53]

As the acts of violence increased in frequency and intensity, Hebert leveled a fair share of the blame for the magnitude of some of the disturbances on officialdom. Referring to some local officials as well as some national figures, he said:

> Those in authority are weak. Those in authority have failed to come up to the standards of their sworn oath of office to support the Constitution and enforce the law.[54]

In addition, he cautioned those politicians who would court radical movements in a desperate hope of cornering a few votes at election time.

> I think, politicalwise, anybody who will advocate, or will associate themselves with these demonstrations . . . these disgraceful demonstrations, if he is in public life, he is in political trouble. . . .[55]

Then, as the riotous excesses of the summer of 1967 descended upon the country, and the majority of the white and black communities stood in shocked horror of what was happening, Hebert expressed what was being felt by millions of Americans across the land. He said:

> The riots in our cities have gone beyond the concept of civil rights. The riots have become revolutions in each part of the country. . . . We wouldn't have had these riots if the Administration had not condoned and urged people to violate the civil laws of the States.[56]

Indeed, this was but the continuation of his criticism of the way in which the Johnson Administration was reacting to the widespread violence. In May, 1967, the Congressman leveled a verbal barrage at the Administration, particularly the Department of Justice. He said:

> The reason that nothing is being done about the Carmichaels and that ilk . . . who are causing bloodshed in this country, who are preaching hatred and bigotry throughout the nation, who are attempting to raise up our black brothers who have done such a magnificent job in this war [Vietnam] and who are patriots, the reason you don't have anything done about it is simple. The Department of Justice has told the American people that it does not

intend to prosecute the laws of the United States which are on the books at the present time.[57]

The Johnson Administration was not, however, solely to blame. The problem had begun to materialize long before that. During an interview with Bill Dickinson for Radio Station WDSU, New Orleans, Hebert traced back to the Eisenhower Administration the genesis of the problem.

> Had these demonstrations, under the guise of civil rights or whatever guise they wanted to call them at that time [1957], been stopped immediately and the violators and so-called non-violence propaganda programs been brought to account, you would not have the riots that you have today.[58]

Still another verbal broadside was leveled at those who had for years gone around preaching that the enactment of civil rights legislation would be a solution to the race problem. Thus, a considerable amount of so-called civil rights legislation was passed by Congress during the 1960's. Congressman Hebert described the effects of this legislation and defined the end product. In July, 1967, he said:

> We have more so-called civil rights legislation on the books of this country than we've ever had in history. These so-called civil rights laws were to be a solution for everything. We were told that if we give these people this and give these people that, we're not going to have any problem. Yet, with more civil rights laws on the books today, we have the greatest span of race riots that this nation has ever known.[59]

Nine months after making the above statement, as large sections of Washington, D. C. lay in smoldering ruin and the situation in many of the other great cities of the land verged on anarchy, Hebert again returned to the theme of civil rights legislation and sought to discover what was accomplished by it.

> We have more riots, we have more unrest, we have more bigotry, we have more prejudice since the first civil rights law was put on the books than we ever had in the history of this nation. And legislation is not going to change the hearts and minds of men.

I have been saying that for years. Education and understanding will be the only solution to the problem which we must all admit is here.[60]

For years Hebert had defended education and understanding as the only true and lasting solution for racial problems (see above, p. 57). Twenty years before these events were taking place, at the dawn of the present civil rights era, Hebert told a radio audience:

When you take a look at the natural born heritage of any race or group, it is very important that just passing a law is not going to make people equal.

But if we are honest and sincere . . . we certainly don't need ambiguous laws to make us be kind and fair to our fellow man— that should come from the heart.[61]

This nation has prided itself since independence on having a government of laws, and Hebert has a healthy respect for the law of the land. Perhaps, then, this accounts for his impatience in reacting to President Johnson's decision to name a commission to investigate the causes of violence in America. Referring to the commission, Hebert said,

Of course, the commission will have very elaborate exercises and come up with a very elaborate report, but I am sure that many of you who have heard me express myself on many occasions share my opinion that the solution is very, very simple to [the problem of] crime in the streets. In three words it can be summed up—*Enforce the law.*[62]

Hebert's concern for the growing lawlessness in the country entered into an address to the student body of Nicholls High School. He said:

[You are] witnessing today the rule of anarchy in your country; you are witnessing the lawlessness of the prohibition era . . . when fear ruled. We live by fear today, and that's not the America into which I was born, and I hope to God that it is not the America in which I will die and [thus] have failed you.[63]

In June, 1968, as the country entered a summer of lawlessness,

Mr. Hebert used the occasion of the tragic death of Senator
Robert F. Kennedy to emphasize the need for a return to law
and order. He said:

> [The assassination of Senator Kennedy] focuses up more sharply,
> and makes it more crystal clear, the necessity of returning law
> and order to this nation which too long has bordered on the
> fringes of anarchy.[64]

As the civil disorders reached a new high in intensity, Hebert
offered to those who would listen a solution for the immediate
problem. On Independence Day, 1967, he urged his listeners

> . . . to return to the garden variety of patriotism. We need a
> simple down-to-earth patriotism.[65]

Such was the simple formula for peace in our times, yet it was
one that was increasingly overshadowed by the shrill voices of
pro and con that screamed and struck and burned and looted.

A short time later, after being escorted into the House of Representatives by armed soldiers, and after watching the smoke of a
burning capital city, Hebert told his constituents:

> There is only one solution for the future. That men of good-
> will on both sides shall abhor and denounce any sort of statement,
> exhibition or demonstration which will lead to lawlessness.[66]

Truly, what a young Congressman Hebert had said so many
years before was still applicable in the late 1960's. In 1945 Hebert
had urged his radio listeners to always remember that

> The basic foundation of true democracy is the rule of the ma-
> jority with full recognition of the rights and the dignity of the
> minority.[67]

CHAPTER III

INTERNATIONAL RELATIONS

As has been indicated, F. Edward Hebert maintains an abiding devotion to America and Americanism. Chapter II focused upon his statements within the general framework of America and Americanism, thus placing special emphasis on the domestic scene. Chapter III will shift the emphasis to America and her relationships with other nations of the earth.

Since 1945, if not before that precise date, it has been a certainty that the United States has had to play a key role in the matter of international relations. Just at the moment when our country emerged as a world leader, another country, the Soviet Union, also evolved into a position of world leadership. Indeed, one might say that the last half of the twentieth century belongs to the United States and Soviet Russia in much the same way that the nineteenth century was the century of Great Britain. The most unfortunate aspect of this evolving two-power world is that the international giants are highly suspicious rivals. Their antagonism is built upon a jealous competition of economic and political systems—a competition that frequently reaches the flash point, as in the case of Korea and Vietnam.

This most volatile contest between the two powers might not be considered dangerous by some observers were it not for two factors that have set man at the crossroads of his destiny. Those two factors are, of course, atomic energy and rocket development. Employing atomic energy or rocket propulsion for peaceful purposes insures mankind of a brilliant future. But dabbling with this technology in a game of military brinkmanship could prove fatal to every living creature on earth.

In this chapter on international relations, the author seeks to indicate how, from the very beginning of the two-power world in 1945, F. Edward Hebert recognized the Soviet Union as the single greatest foreign threat to democracy; the dangers to mankind of atomic warfare; and, finally, the alarming effects of the US-USSR confrontation around the world.

On War, Peace, Isolation, and Collective Security

In the pre-Vietnam days, one often heard of the isolation sentiment to be found in particular areas of the United States. Indeed, in the late 1960's, there was reviving something that might be called neo-isolation, as various groups of youngsters and oldsters paraded their anti-war and anti-involvement sentiments. Isolationism is an old element in American life and its acceptance was, perhaps, legitimately debatable until 1945. Since then, however, only the politically naive can fail to recognize the destiny of America's unenviable world position. Mr. Hebert expressed himself on the subject of isolation shortly after the second Great War. He said:

> A familiar chant goes up around the country this time of year, from those who would pull our two oceans up around us and have us live as a solitary nation.
>
> These people consistently back up this contention with one of the famous quotations from the Farewell Address of George Washington. . . .
>
> But this is 1954. . . .
>
> America, as well as every other country of the world, depends on contact with the others for its very livelihood. How, then, can we isolate ourselves between our two oceans and pretend the rest of the world does not exist.
>
> We cannot. . . .
>
> Basically, Washington's advice still holds good. We must not engage in alliances with other countries that would commit us to a course of action that is not in our own best interests. We must not, for example, obligate ourselves to go to war because a local civil war breaks out in Asia.[1]

Because he appreciates America's destiny in the second half of
the twentieth century, Hebert has, since entering Congress on the
eve of World War II, argued in favor of political, economic and,
above all, military preparedness. At the conclusion of World War
II, and significantly on the second anniversary of D-Day, he uttered the one sentence that has been his guideline on the subject of
preparedness ever since. He told a radio audience:

> The nation which is best prepared to fight a war is the nation
> which will keep longest the peace.[2]

Few of our national leaders, however, heeded these words from
the congressman from Louisiana. Indeed, many of them believed
that Russo-American relations after World War II would remain
in a suspended honeymoon stage. By 1948 these trusting American
politicians had been almost lured into the Russian trap. Just after
the fall of Czechoslovakia to communism, Hebert verbally attacked those trusting souls who believed that the Communists
would play the game of international politics according to Western rules.

> Isn't it a pity and a shame that we have allowed Communism to
> spread as far as it has, and to impose the rule of minorities upon
> majorities to such an extent that the President of the United States
> finds it necessary to beat the drums of war to rally a nation and a
> world to the cause of peace.
> The tragedy is that the leaders of this nation have only now
> realized and expressed publicly what I warned about almost three
> years ago. Certainly if I, your congressman, could foresee these
> events, these men who surround the President of the United
> States must, too, have been able to see what would happen if we
> demobilized our army, wrapped up our navy in mothballs, and
> grounded our air force. What happened, and is now taking place,
> is not unexpected of those of us who saw communism and the
> action of Russia firsthand. . . .[3]

In addition to being prepared by having sufficient military
hardware, Hebert believes it necessary to prepare in still another
way. In this instance he is one of the few men of our times who

has linked war with incompetent leadership. Speaking on the subject of "The Historic Futility of Wars to End Wars," the Congressman said:

> The futility and the tragedy of what has gone before lies not in the failure of the little people whose sons obeyed orders and battled in mortal combat, but in the failure of the big men who assumed the leadership of the little people. Theirs was the failure and theirs will be the responsibility when the book of judgment is balanced.
>
> If we are to survive, if America is to live, we should demand men of stature, honor and integrity and accept nothing less. Men's lives are too sacred to be used as chips on the political poker table of ambitious men.[4]

Not only must America have the very best in leadership, but, says Hebert, we must withdraw from the naive pattern of diplomacy to which this country adhered in its pre-great-power days.

> We have always assumed that everyone else is going to play the game according to the rules in the book. We go into every international conference like it is a church social and then we're surprised and hurt when we discover we're actually caught in a den of international thugs and cutthroats.[5]

But if diplomacy fails in its purpose and uncontrollable factors lead America into war, the nation must have leaders who will face up to the realities of the situation. Indeed, when the subject of war is raised, F. Edward Hebert takes his stand as a realist—as one who clearly recognizes in war the antithesis of idealism. Perhaps this common-sense approach to the subject arises from the fact that Hebert witnessed the "war to end all wars" and its aftermath. Perhaps his realism is based upon his awareness of the debacle of the League of Nations, and, now, the frustrations of the United Nations. The fact remains, nevertheless, that whenever Hebert has addressed himself to the subject of war, he has employed calm, well-measured words, demonstrative of his realistic attitude.

Six weeks before the infamy of Pearl Harbor, Hebert voiced confidence in America's foreign policy as enunciated by the Roosevelt Administration. He was of the opinion that the President and his advisors were employing every human skill to keep war away from our shores. Nevertheless, the Congressman's realism surfaced when he said:

> Since the Garden of Eden human nature has not changed. There will be war on the face of the earth as long as there are two men alive. We can't totally eliminate war but we can hold it to a minimum and take every means available to keep war away from our shores.[6]

Then, after nearly four years of war, he addressed his constituents saying:

> We must be realistic and recognize the fact that this is not going to be the last war to be fought. Wars have been fought as long as there are two nations to face one another. We cannot prevent wars, but we can take definite and positive steps to reduce their number.[7]

On May 24, 1945, during a congressional investigating team's tour of war-torn Europe, Hebert wrote:

> Why can't Americans be more realistic in this whole business [of war]?
> If only we had been more realistic after the last war, we would not have had to come back here again twenty-five years later to do all over and at a greater cost of life, what we had done before. It has been only repetition with emphasis—death and destruction being used for the emphasis.[8]

Again, in 1950, shortly after the outbreak of the Korean conflict, Hebert intoned that:

> Any kind of war, a cold war or a hot war, is dirty business. The ledger is never balanced in war. Everybody loses. The object is simply to lose less than your opponent.[9]

Then, during the Vietnamese conflict, as anti-war demonstrations swept America, Hebert recalled a simple fact that perhaps has eluded many Americans of a less realistic persuasion. In a

speech to the student body of Nicholls High School in New Orleans, the Congressman said:

> War is an awful thing. But we must remember that we are free
> today because of the Revolutionary War and that we are one na-
> tion today because of the Civil War.[10]

These are thought-provoking words and Hebert has used com-
parable language when discussing the functions of the United
Nations as a deterrent of war.

> Today there is much doubt that it does, because of its failure to
> stand resolutely behind its own actions when adversity stalks the
> highway.[11]

The above statement was not made with reference to the situation in the Congo during the early 1960's, although it could be
accurately applied to that situation. The statement was not made
in connection with the Middle East situation of the late 1960's,
although it appears tailor-made for that troubled area. The statement, as valid today as the day it was uttered, was made on February 10, 1951, with regard to the lack of action on the part of
U. N. members following the invasion of Korea by Chinese Communists. At the time Mr. Hebert explained the frequent duplicity
of the United Nations. He said:

> When the tide of defeat on the Korean peninsula was turned
> into a march of victory by the American solider, the members of
> the U. N. stood solidly behind America.
>
> Then came the day of reverses when Red China's hordes swept
> over the Yalu River and routed America's forces in one of this
> nation's most tragic military defeats.
>
> Almost overnight the complexion of the U. N. changed.
>
> Boldness was supplanted by timidity and America had to fight
> for support of the ideals for which she had fought at the behest
> of those who now stood ready to desert her.[12]

As the years have passed in the history of the United Nations,
Hebert's realistic evaluation of that body's effectiveness as a deterrent of war is in no way altered. On June 25, 1967, just after

the events of the Six Day War between Israel and the Arab states, the Congressman told a television audience:

I have always said that the United Nations is, at best, a ladies sewing circle or nice debating club.[13]

In another area of international relations, Hebert's realistic attitude and appreciation of existing circumstances have developed in him a straightforward approach to the attempt occasionally made by the United States government to influence the destiny of other nations. During some of the darkest days of World War II, Hebert said:

The right of self-determination is the right of all people, and it is just as much our business to see that Germany has the right of self-determination, and Russia, and France, whether it is communism they want or whatever, and to protect the right of any of our friends, as it is to protect our own right of self-determination.[14]

Hebert's abiding confidence in the ability of a nation to determine for itself the most beneficial political and economic system has been stated in the following terms:

I simply do not subscribe to the idea that we have the right to impose a so-called democratic type government on other people any more than they have a right to impose dictatorship on us.[15]

True, after World War II, with the introduction of the concept of foreign aid, Hebert supported the Marshall plan for European economic recovery, but his support of the program was based upon the fact that

Financial support to other nations should be treated with the same caution as subsidy in our own country. There has got to be a stop somewhere down the line. . . . Remember, friendship can't be bought with dollars and cents.[16]

This perceptible approach to international relations and international friendship did not mean, however, that Hebert was oblivious to the universal suffering of Europeans following World War II. Indeed he, himself, told of the heart-rendering scenes of misery and despair in postwar Europe in his book entitled *I Went, I Saw, I Heard*.[17] A year after the war's conclusion, remembering the emaciated children of Europe, F. Edward Hebert delivered one of the finest speeches of his career. He entitled it "Feeding the World." Below are some excerpts from that speech which he delivered to his constituents over radio on the evening of May 30, 1946. Certainly, in each of the selected statements that follow, the great humanitarian spirit that wells up in this man is clearly discernable.

America must fight the war against famine in order to win the struggle for peace.

Men and women dazed by hunger do not listen to clearly reasoned explanations, they cannot eat arguments in newspapers.

Famine, chaos, riot, disorder, anarchy, death, war . . . [grow] from the seeds of starvation that are putting down roots in the world today.

You have always thought that it takes police to keep order. But we know now that police cannot keep order unless people are fed. It takes an average of 2200 calories a day to keep order.

Liberty is a necessity only to people who have bread.[18]

These are words that have hung heavy with the truth of the ages. Only a man of vision—only a man who knows and understands the individual drives of other men—only a man of compassion—could see the fatigue, despair, and utter hopelessness of most Europeans. Thus, Hebert was well aware in 1946 that if Western Europe was to be saved for the democratic world, salvation would begin with a crust of bread.

Western Europe, however, had to be saved on several fronts. Starvation was not the only menace. So many people failed to see the danger signals light up as international communism recognized an excellent opportunity in the victory of Soviet Russia to spread beyond the frontiers of that tormented land. So many Washington politicians continued to believe that the diplomatic honeymoon with the Russians would continue after the final defeat of Hitler.

Hebert, on the other hand, took note of the danger signals and warned of the threat. Two weeks after V-E Day he wrote:

The ideologies of Americans and Russians are as divergent . . . as the poles. Because there is such a difference of opinion, however, is no bar to mutual respect and understanding but the two ends will never meet. Hoping, wishing, stargazing and dreaming will not change overnight that which has been imbedded in the various peoples of the world.[19]

Less than a year after V-E Day, Hebert attached the following addendum to his warning.

The noise that each day grows more deafening in our ears is the growl of the Russian bear.[20]

There were those people who continued to believe that old-fashioned diplomacy would serve to settle the differences in Soviet-American relations. Hebert was not among that group of naive individuals. He pointed out that

At the peace table it will be learned that Russia is going to attempt for the largest pieces of the pie. Because we do not believe in grabbing any part of the pie will not deter Russia from attempting to grab pie, crust, plate and everything on it.[21]

As Soviet-American relations cooled in the diplomatic chill of the immediate post-war years and, then, became frigid with the first Russian invasion of Czechoslovakia in February, 1948, Hebert again emphasized the Russian menace to a free Europe. He said:

We must meet the Russians on the only ground on which Russians walk—Power!
There will be no trouble with Russia in the future if we determine to talk with Russia across the table with all the cards face up. Russia knows and understands the language of power and realism.[22]

If one but pauses to think of the Berlin Blockade, Korea, and the Cuban missile crisis, can one doubt the validity of Hebert's advice? A week after making the above statement, the Congressman was again before the microphone discussing Soviet-American relations. It was during the course of this speech that he first mentioned the term "cold war." The importance of the speech, however, lies in the deep insight into Soviet-American relations which the Congressman exhibited. He said:

> Nobody imagines that at any future moment there will be a spectacular overall 'settlement' between the United States and the Soviet Union. 'Settlement' if it comes, will be a long and tedious process, starting with agreement on some small issue and then proceeding to agreement on others over the years.[23]

Following the Berlin Blockade, an episode in which the Russian bear was forced to back away from the united stand of the Western Allies, and the subsequent formation of the North Atlantic Treaty Organization, Hebert reminded his constituents that sugary diplomacy is not always the proper approach when dealing with the Russians. He said:

> My only hope at the moment is that we deal with Russia not in the language of trust which is not understood but in the language of might which the Russians understand so well.[24]

It is Hebert's opinion that if America loses the diplomatic contest to Russia, our diplomats will have no one but themselves to blame. He once wrote:

> I [cannot] blame Russia for trying to get all it can at the peace table . . . but I will lay the blame at the door of America if our diplomats allow Molotov or whoever represents Russia, to get away with it.[25]

The spring thaw of 1953 brought with it an apparent thaw in Soviet-American relations following the death of Joseph Stalin. Many persons thought that an entirely new era in Russo-American relations was on the verge of dawning. Perhaps now, they speculated, the sabre-rattling would go away. During a discussion of the thought-to-be peace gestures of the Russians, Hebert said:

> So long as millions of captive peoples live under the heel of

Moscow's tyranny, there can be no reliance on Russian 'anti-war' propaganda. . . .

The peace of the world still depends on the strength and unity of the free nations, who relax at their own peril.[26]

In time, particularly with the formation of NATO, there was forged a military arm of the free nations that could match that of the Russian militarists. The threat to democratic institutions, however, did not subside. Certainly the action being taken against those institutions was not as overt as it had been for the past few years in Eastern Europe, but action was being taken not only in Western Europe but also in the United States. The action was predicated upon the belief that what could not be taken by the sword might fall by the word—by a subtle dissemination of communist ideology. This transition was well noted by the members of the Un-American Activities Committee of the House of Representatives. Serving on that committee in the late 1940's, Hebert, like so many of his colleagues, tried to warn their fellow countrymen of the subtleties and scope of communist subversion.

Once, after having questioned Elizabeth Bentley concerning her turn to communism, Hebert tried to answer the question that so many of his constituents were asking: Why does an American become a communist? The Congressman drew upon Bentley's testimony in answering the question. He said:

> When I asked her [Bentley] concerning her elementary education she said that she had never really been instructed in the principles of this government and knew little of what it meant to be an American. This is not the fault of the Bentleys but it is the fault of our educators at whose door must be placed the blame for this shocking condition. The complacency of too many otherwise loyal Americans to the benefits of our system of government can be traced directly to a lack of education. Communism thrives and grows abundantly in a field of ignorance.[27]

A year later, after hearing more testimony from witnesses before the Un-American Activities Committee, Hebert was able to expand upon his earlier statement. He said:

> Most people who join with the communists appear to do so

for reasons they believe to be idealistic. This, coupled with a sense of frustration, for some reason or another, is believed to be the motivating influence which leads many average and prosperous Americans to become associated and involved in the communist movement.[28]

In recent years Mr. Hebert has added still another dimension to his explanation of why an American can be converted to communism. Once more, one discovers that the Congressman's opinion is based upon a most realistic appraisal of recent events. He recognizes the fact that many individuals embrace communism for no other reason than their belief that it is a road to power—a way to control other men.

The North Atlantic Treaty Organization became, as implied earlier, the instrument of containment of communist territorial expansion in Europe. This alliance of the Western democracies brought an eager response from Congressman Hebert. He said:

> A bright and shining new chapter in the progressive history of freedom in America was written here in Washington last week with the signing of the North Atlantic Treaty.[29]

Indeed, the alliance brought a feeling of security not only to those who, like Hebert, had seen the Russian trap made ready for the enslavement of all Europe but also to the millions of non-communists throughout the Western world. Events of recent years, particularly the Greek civil war, the communist *coup d'etat* in Czechoslovakia, the Berlin Blockade, and the communist challenge at the polls in the Italian elections, have caused many non-communists in Western Europe to wonder if the defeat of the Nazi dictatorship only meant enslavement under the Soviet dictatorship. As early as 1945, during his European trip, Hebert recognized the communist threat to Italy. At the time he wrote:

> Italy has six political parties and once again the best organized are the Communists, and the finger of organization points in the direction of the Kremlin.[30]

As Western Europe moved into the post-war era, Congressman

Hebert became quite anxious for the future of Italy. On three occasions in the spring of 1948 he spoke to his constituents concerning the forthcoming elections in Italy. He knew well that many of his friends and supporters in the New Orleans area were of Italian descent, and therefore felt that if he could tell them of the consequences of a communist victory at the Italian polls, they, in turn, would urge their friends and relatives in Italy to vote for the non-communist parties.[31]

The non-communist parties did win that election. Italy, and particularly the large Italian Communist party, did, nevertheless, remain a matter of concern for Mr. Hebert. In 1954, after the fall of Premier Fanfani's government, the Congressman interpreted the situation in Italy as being a threat to the Western defense system. He said:

> The failure of Premier Fanfani to obtain a vote of confidence for his government constitutes a serious danger to Italian participation in the Western defense program. Unless the crisis is solved, Italy will have another general election.
> A communist Italy at the backdoor of France, threatening all the Mediterranean, would wreck European defense plans.[32]

Hebert, therefore, was not convinced of Russian sincerity when the Big Four foreign ministers met in Berlin in early 1954. Indeed, the Congressman felt that Russia was using the Big Four meeting in a grandstand play to foist upon the world old cliches about peace and world disarmament. He sought to go behind the Russian facade to discover their real objective. Hebert reported to his constituents:

> Their aim [the Russians] is to scuttle the united European army project on which the United States has based its foreign policy. They want to create disunity and dissatisfaction among the nations of Western Europe and split them off from their allies.
> Specifically, the Russians want to cut off France, who is already wavering and unstable. France was the originator of the European army plan; yet she has not ratified the treaty and is showing increasing coldness toward it.

Molotov is playing on this indecision. If the Soviets can appear hospitable to France, if they can convince the French they can evolve peace without the army plan, then it is lost for all time.[33]

A short time later Hebert reported to his constituents that the foreign ministers' meeting in Berlin had come to nothing. Furthermore, Molotov's plan for the future of Germany was unacceptable to the Western allies. Hebert emphasized the fact, however, that

> The wily Molotov has a sleeper up his sleeve that he hasn't fully revealed yet. He's got his eye on France, which is the weak sister in the Western European defense alliance. In an effort to swing France away from her allies and over to his side, Molotov has been dropping some subtle hints about Indo-China.[34]

The subtle hints had to do with the fact that if France would go along with Moscow on the European defense alliance, Moscow would order a negotiated peace in the then eight-year-old Indo-China war. Would the French take the bait? That was difficult to say. Hebert would say, however, that

> The French are sick and tired of that unpopular war that is being fought in steaming jungle and is draining off Frenchmen, arms, and money. Draining off our money, too, incidentally, since we have promised substantial aid to France to fight the Indo-China war.[35]

France, Hebert feared, would therefore be willing to talk about Indo-China with the Russians at the first indication of the Communists' good intentions.

Soviet subtleties are usually but a thin veneer that can be easily penetrated by Western negotiators and observers. Beneath that veneer is the ever-present desire by most communist leaders to seize by force of arms what is unobtainable through negotiations. Indeed, in the years since 1945, the communists of the world have been far more inclined to get what they want through violence, death, misery and war, than they have through discussions and serious negotiations. To recall but a few incidents of communist violence, by way of example, there were the Berlin and Polish uprisings of 1953 that were crushed by Russian armed strength. These episodes were followed by the rape of Hungary in 1956, the betrayal of the hopes of the Cuban people in 1959, and the unforgivable interference in the domestic affairs of Czechoslovakia in 1968. But the two great episodes of death-dealing communist violence since 1950 have occurred in Korea and Vietnam.

The thought has occurred to some people that the twenty-year wave of communist violence may be due in large measure to the development of an atomic arsenal. On the other hand, some observers contend that the development of these atomic stockpiles by both East and West has prevented a third world war. At any rate, mankind has, in the period since World War II, become acutely conscious of the "bomb."

On the Bomb

F. Edward Hebert, as a member of the Armed Services Committee of the House of Representatives, has always maintained a keen interest in the use of atomic energy. His interest stems, in large measure, from a deep desire to see atomic energy used for peaceful purposes. The following excerpts, taken from the Congressman's speeches on the subject of atomic energy, will clearly demonstrate his respect for the power of the atom as well as his desire to see that power harnessed for the benefit of mankind.

Less than a year after the atomic tests in New Mexico, Congressman Hebert was able to report to his constituents that he had had a preview of the American fleet "of tomorrow." He told his listeners that he had heard of marvelous plans for atomic-propelled ships, extensive use of guided missiles and, he said:

> There is every prospect of a radically new type submarine probably employing atomic energy—which will proceed for weeks at a time completely submerged at higher speeds than our present subs.[36]

Man has long dreamed of the peaceful uses of atomic energy to drive his ships, turn his mills and make simple a multitude of other tasks associated with the need for energy. There is, however, another side of the atomic energy story—one that man cannot ignore.

He cannot ignore the fact that atomic energy can end all life on the planet. Conscious of the grim consequences of the abuse of atomic energy, Hebert has long been in the forefront of those individuals who wish to inform not only Americans but all mankind of the potential of atomic power. Hebert told a radio audience:

> The atomic bomb is no pop-gun. It is a terrible weapon of mass destruction, and the world should know it. . . .
> And so should the American people. Our people should be told not only the potential of our atomic stockpile but also the approximate strength of Russian nuclear power.[37]

For many years Congressman Hebert has urged that our scientists and those individuals charged with the responsibility of developing atomic power should not become obsessed with its use only as a weapon. On one occasion he said:

> In our concentration on the war-like influences of the world today, we must not forget that atomic energy offers a constructive challenge. Let's not forget that the atom can be put to use in peacetime to better the status of mankind.
> In our eagerness to destroy or eliminate evil, let's not lose sight of the peacetime potential of the atom.[38]

Then, after witnessing the firing of the newly developed atomic cannon, the Congressman told his constituents:

> Times and weapons have changed since the slingshot was first used centuries ago, but the nature of man has not changed. . . .
> The ultimate objective remains the same—death, kill, destroy, destroy, kill. . . .
> If only the creative genius of man could be directed to construction instead of destruction.
> When will the newly discovered science of the atomic age be turned in the direction of peace instead of war.
> How long can this civilization last with man continually planning, scheming, conniving and plotting to kill or be killed? [39]

Prior to the test firing of the atomic cannon, Congressman Hebert witnessed the nuclear blast at Eniwetok. He described that holocaust in these words:

When I saw the shot at Eniwetok I said I had a feeling that I was standing at the gates of hell looking into that firey eternity.... [Hebert wondered] Is tomorrow a prelude to the beginning of the end of civilization? [40]

Perhaps because of these two sobering experiences with atomic tests, Mr. Hebert has consistently emphasized the need for frank and open discussions concerning the nature and destructive potential of atomic weaponry. He believes that the greatest disaster which could befall mankind would be for one of the atomic powers to underestimate the military strength of another, and thereby blunder into a war that could do irreparable harm to mankind. His opinions have prompted him to say:

It is time we let the Soviets know the full extent and potential of our atomic power. It's time we told them that we have the retaliatory power to strike back. That would prevent Russia from blundering into a war because they underestimated our atomic strength.[41]

Mr. Hebert's primary concern, however, the goal toward which he expended so much effort, is the peaceful application of atomic energy. Toward this end he has said:

Until the unlimited powers of atomic energy are converted to its vast peace potential, we cannot hope for peace in our time.[42]

As the seemingly endless arms race of mankind increased in tempo after World War II, as Russia and the United States tested larger and more destructive atomic devices during the course of the 1950's, Hebert gave expression to the thoughts of many men when he spoke of a reasonable limitation being placed upon the use of these death-dealing instruments. Hence, fully ten years before the conclusion of the Test Ban Treaty between the United States and Soviet Russia, Hebert said:

March 1, 1954 ... may well go down in our books as the turning point of modern history. That was the day when a thermonuclear bomb was exploded....

This explosion was about 600 times as powerful as the Hiroshima atomic bomb....

As we read more and more about the latest Pacific tests, [we] must realize the magnitude of the problem now confronting us.

Attempts to outlaw atomic weapons will certainly increase as a result of the new power displayed on March 1.

The urge will be to define and limit the circumstances in which it can be used, with the hope of obtaining the kind of balance which forestalled use of poisonous gas in the last war [World War II].

This is a challenge which faces the leaders of all nations. Or at least the nations which hope to survive and, although Russia acts at times as if it had no interest in surviving, when the final payoff comes, the urge to live will come to the forefront.[43]

It has taken time for the two superpowers in the East-West confrontation to realize the danger threatening the survival of mankind. The Test Ban Treaty and the start of the arms limitation talks in Helsinki and Vienna (the so-called S.A.L.T. talks between Russia and the United States) do bear witness to Mr. Hebert's proposition that, despite all the sabre-rattling, there is an inherent desire in man to survive.

On Korea

Congressman Hebert's thoughts concerning the awesome power of atomic energy and the misery and death that abuse of that power could bring upon mankind were frequent during the early 1950's. And rightfully so, for these were the years of the Korean conflict. These were the years when men who believed that the United Nations had a meaningful function tried to make that function a reality. Thus, when South Korea was invaded by North Korean troops in June, 1950, those people who favored the collective action of the United Nations in halting an act of aggression felt that the time had come for that organization to prove its mettle. It was, therefore, with more than just a sense of disappointment that some people came to realize that not only were many U.N. members opposed to joint action against an aggressor but, indeed, they were determined to wreck the collaborative scheme.

Simultaneously, the Truman Administration decided to commit the United States armed forces for the defense of South Korea. This action was put into effect to such a degree that the American presence in Korea far overshadowed that of any other nation which had elected to meaningfully oppose aggression.

Less than a month after the beginning of the Korean hostilities, Mr. Hebert gave vent to some thoughts that were pertinent not only to that particular time but also to the future.

> I am one of those who believe that the fight in Korea is the world's fight—it is not only America's fight. I am one of those who believe that everyone of the members of the United Nations should contribute its share of fighting men to the common cause. I do not believe in only American boys dying while crowded grandstands of other nations cheer the fighting spirit and the courage of Americans. . . .
>
> I have never advocated that America attempt to save the world unless saving the world redound to the protection and security of America.[44]

At the same time, Mr. Hebert spoke of something which indicates that his thinking was far in advance of many of his contemporaries, even his colleagues on the Hill. Certainly, in the years since the Korean conflict, great consideration has been given to the following concept which Hebert expressed in 1950.

> Korea has a civilization of its own which has existed for four thousand years and a foreign power simply can't walk into such a civilization and say authoritatively: 'It's time you change your system of government and adopt our ideas of democracy.' [45]

In Hebert's world of political reality, there has never been a moment's doubt that the imposition of the veneer of democracy does not necessarily result in a democratic nation.

The Korean conflict dragged on for three years with American men and American taxpayers supporting the greatest burden of the fight. By the time of the first Eisenhower inauguration, many Americans were asking the question: "What are we doing in Korea? Will the war ever end?" They had a right to ask these questions as the truce talks which had begun in 1952 were nearly

a year old. In April, 1953, Mr. Hebert summed up American
thinking, and, in doing so, spoke words as applicable to the situation in South Vietnam in the summer of 1969 as they were applicable to the situation in Korea in 1953. He said:

> Americans were optimistic when the truce talks began in Korea
> more than a year ago. They hoped for a cessation of war which
> was not popular because the fundamental issues involved were
> neither understood nor comprehended by the people who gath-
> ered at the drug store on Main Street.[46]

Then, of course, came the frustration that surrounded the Korean conflict. In the following statement Mr. Hebert expresses the
sense of frustration so keenly felt by a large number of Americans
and adds a comment about the political bungling that led to war.
Furthermore, he warns once more against permitting politicians
to use American troops as pawns.

> The Korean war will forever stand in American history as a
> monumental example of indecision, bewilderment, confusion, and
> downright stupidity.
> It never should have happened. It could have been prevented,
> but having happened it became the first war perhaps in all civil-
> ization whereby the potential winner was under instructions not
> to win. The tragedy was that politicians were permitted to use
> human lives as pawns on the international chessboard.[47]

In his usual forthright manner, Mr. Hebert has consistently attacked those men who would let Americans die in distant lands
while playing politics at home. On occasion his comments have
related directly to the leaders of his own party, but this has not
prevented Hebert from expressing his views. In March, 1953, he
said:

> The Roosevelt and Truman administrations covered up the
> sell-out deals so carefully throughout the years, that only now is
> their full significance beginning to emerge. . . .
> The United States paid an enormous price at Yalta to get Russia
> into the Far Eastern war [at the end of World War II]. American
> boys are still paying off that deal on the battlefields of Korea.[48]

Thus, for most Americans, the Korean conflict dragged to an

end on a note of gloom. The only bright spot in the armistice agreement was that American men would no longer be dying for a piece of real estate that was virtually impossible to retain should the Red Chinese decide to take it. Nevertheless, the prevailing opinion was that the country could settle down to domestic problems, and young Americans could plan their future.

What most Americans could not know was that as the Korean conflict was coming to an end, events elsewhere in Asia were developing that would ultimately cost a great sacrifice in human life and human effort. At the moment, the mid-1950's, Americans knew of the place as Indo-China, but another name for part of the area was beginning to creep into conversations. Now and then one heard of Vietnam.

On the War in Indo-China

The French and the peoples of Indo-China reached a climax in their struggle for that tortured land in the 1950's. The struggle of the natives, however, was not simply a nationalist struggle to free the country from colonial rule, for there was a definite strain of communism mixed with the spirit of nationalism. In the late 1940's the Red tide had flowed across China, and no one with any real knowledge of communism expected for a moment that the onrushing tide of communist victory would suddenly stop at the borders of Southeast Asia. It was only the war in Korea (which was little more than the overflow of Chinese armies from victory in their own land) that prevented a definitive settlement in Indo-China. By 1953, however, with a truce in Korea freeing thousands of Chinese troops and, more importantly, valuable equipment, it seemed as though there was remarkably little to prevent a communist takeover of Southeast Asia. Recognizing the developing crisis in Indo-China, Hebert, in May, 1953, spoke of the type of assistance that the United States should give the French in Southeast Asia. He was also most emphatic concerning what assistance should be withheld. He said:

> The Free World must take a stand against aggression in Southeast Asia.

The French defenders of Indo-China must be aided . . . . [with] weapons of war to shore up this out-post of freedom in the East.

But the line must be drawn against sending American troops. Not a single drop of American blood shall be spilled in Laos to stop the communist advance.

America has always answered their [the French] cries for help. In fact, usually, we have answered not only with money and equipment, but with our soldiers as well. We have given those foreign nations both the tools and the men.

That's got to stop. . . .

It's time the rest of the world contributed some of its own manpower in the united crusade against communism. . . .

American manhood is not expendable.

The most serious mistake this nation could make would be to over-extend ourselves. If we pour troops into Laos, Thailand, Burma, and all the other troubled spots of the world, we run the risk of ripping the pillars of strength from under our own country.

I am not minimizing the threat that stalks the Free World today. I am thinking of the future—of the long, hard pull ahead—and the need we will have in the future for clear-thinking, hard-hitting leadership.

And our future leaders are those American boys who are climbing into military uniform today.

Their survival is this country's survival.[49]

This insight into the problem of Southeast Asia was not a happenstance. Several months later Hebert further interpreted developments in the Southeast Asian conflict and stated the possible consequences. He said:

The French are sick and tired of that unpopular war that is being fought in steaming jungle and is draining off Frenchmen, arms, and money. Draining off our money too, incidentally, since we have promised substantial aid to France to fight the Indo-China war. . . .

The French would like us to take over that jungle war entirely. Why should we? There have been reports—not denied in official quarters in Washington—that we are considering sending several hundred mechanics and maintenance experts over there to help keep French planes flying.

Once we stick our big toe in, the whole foot is bound to follow.[50]

These prophetic words were followed a week later by still another report to the people of Louisiana's First District concerning the subject of the Indo-China war. In the following excerpt one can detect a deep concern for the future. Mr. Hebert said:

There is good reason for the growing concern here in Washington that Indo-China may become another Korea. It is reassuring to have both President Eisenhower and his Secretary of Defense disclaim any such possibility.

However, the danger doesn't come from either the President or the Secretary. There is no one on Capitol Hill who would accuse them of trying to push us into this conflict.

The danger comes from the fact that we may be 'back-doored' into the present Indo-China conflict. . . .

The French government has asked the American government to send additional American technicians and planes. It is reasonable to assume that the next request will be for ground troops.

We have sent some additional technicians to the scene, but we cannot—at the risk of involvement in all-out war—send American planes, pilots and combat troops.

The President has decided to send 400 aircraft maintenance men to Indo-China and, it is within the realm of possibility, that the pressure of these American technicians there could provide the spark for the Reds to lure us further into the war. . . .

The theme of this drive to involve us was offered by a news commentator the other night. He said, 'Can we afford to let Indo-China go communist by default?'

That is one of the opening guns in the effort to 'back-door' us into the present bloody war in Indo-China. It will grow in intensity.

American troops should not—must not—will not—be sent into the Asian conflict.

One Korea in a generation is enough forever.[51]

In mid-April, 1954, Mr. Hebert returned to the subject of Indo-

China in a report to his constituents. He indicated that the United States might aid the French with arms, but concerning the involvement of American troops, Hebert was explicit:

> What can be done about Indo-China?
> What should be done about Indo-China?
> That is the problem the Administration is now wrestling with and, from all the reports, it isn't coming up with any simple answer.
> There just isn't any simple answer to the question of communist expansion in Asia. . . .
> What are we doing to help [the French]?
> We carry the money burden of the war. We send planes and supplies.
> Dare we do more?
> Dare we send in our American troops to fight and die?
> The answer to that is NO. . . .[52]

The Congressman concluded his address by pointing up a fact that few Americans recognized or cared to entertain after the military victories of World War II. Indeed, the fact was not fully recognized by the American political leadership for another fourteen years. Mr. Hebert said:

> The war in Indo-China won't be won by guns, ammunition and troops. That war will only be won by shrewd diplomacy and political maneuvering.[53]

Subsequently, Mr. Hebert returned to the theme that the only solution for the problem of Indo-China was to be found in a political approach. If the communists made their ideology appealing to the man in the street, why, Hebert asked, couldn't the democratic states do the same thing? Once again the Congressman visualized shrewd politics replacing war. He said:

> There is no need for [American] manpower in Indo-China. The natives, if given an incentive to fight, could be trained to meet the threat of communism.[54]

But events in Indo-China were moving swiftly in the late spring of 1954. Matters were going poorly for the French, making it appear that still another area of Asia would fall under communist domination. More and more the question was being heard: "Will the United States intervene?" In answer to that question Hebert told his constituents:

> The back door to war is open.
>
> The question is whether we're going to allow ourselves to be pushed in.
>
> The French are trying with all their might to get us over the threshold of Indo-China. We gave them airplanes. . . . Now they want us to send more planes manned by American crews.
>
> From all informed reports so far, the Administration has rejected the French plea for uniformed American pilots. Yet President Eisenhower and other top Administration officials continue pounding away at the American people on the importance of Dien Bien Phu to our own destiny.
>
> If we take the step of air intervention, we may find ourselves pulled, however unwillingly, into all out intervention.
>
> What good would American intervention do anyway? [55]

Mr. Hebert continued with his thoughts on the consequences of the fall of Indo-China to the communists. He also offered reasons why the United States should not commit troops to that war. The reasons offered by the Congressman in 1954 remain valid a decade and half later. He said:

> The fall of Indo-China would be a serious blow to the free nations. That would leave a clear path for the communists to sweep across Asia and shrink the free world to the Atlantic countries.
>
> But there are equally compelling reasons for our staying *out* of Indo-China.
>
> About sixteen thousand Frenchmen and about forty thousand native troops have been lost in eight years of war in Indo-China. . . .
>
> The combined French Union armed forces far outnumber those of the communist-led Vietminh; their equipment—most of it supplied by us—is far superior.
>
> Why, then, is the war apparently being lost?
>
> One major reason is that the Vietnam government, kept in power by the French, has little popular support. . . .

> Besides, very little real effort has been made to train and equip the Vietnamese into a powerful combat force.[56]

A week later Mr. Hebert touched upon a subject that became a sharp issue between the congressional and executive branches of the government during the last years of the Johnson Administration—the issue of congressional authorization for the commitment of troops to a combat zone.

Concerning this subject, Mr. Hebert said:

> It would be suicidal for Congress to pass any legislation restricting the President's power to send emergency combat forces abroad without specific congressional authorization.
>
> But that does not mean Congress would countenance the use of that power to inch this nation into war. There is a widespread fear across the land today that we might become involved in the Indo-China war without will, wish, or warning.[57]

Almost simultaneously with the utterance of these words Dien Bien Phu was falling to the Vietminh and the representatives of communism and democracy were meeting in Geneva for the partitioning of still another unhappy nation—one-half communist—one-half non-communist.

In early June, 1954, Congressman Hebert noted the fall of Dien Bien Phu and the continuing possibility of the United States getting militarily involved in Southeast Asia. More importantly, he told his radio audience of the situation in Indo-China as it related to international affairs and the people of Indo-China.

> Dien Bien Phu is no longer in the news now that it has fallen. But the problem of Indo-China and what we, the United States, should do about it, is just as urgent as ever.
>
> We are slowly and subtly coming to the day when we must make a decision. We must make that decision on the question: Should American troops be sent into the Indo-China conflict?
>
> The answer would seem to be, at this time, No. And nothing seems likely to happen that could change that answer.
>
> There are, however, certain definite, positive actions that can be taken to ease the present situation in Indo-China without demanding that American boys be sacrificed.

The first, and most obvious, is that France allow this matter to be handled by the United Nations. . . .

Perhaps the greatest good that could come out of turning this affair over to the U. N. would be that a policy could be obtained. The natives, even many of those fighting with the French, claim they want independence.

The natives—and this goes for those fighting with the French—resent the white man, whether he is French, English or American.

These men and women want their freedom. They want their freedom from the rule of the white man under whom they have served for generations.[58]

That was the essence of the problem in Indo-China. The people of that land, in overwhelming numbers, wanted independence. Furthermore, the French position was made even more damning by the fact that they had allowed the communists to seize upon the independence issue and use it for everything it was worth. For this reason, as Hebert well recognized, the problems of Indo-China could not be settled by guns, the only solution was to be found in subtle diplomacy and politics. The United States, however, was not engaging in subtle diplomacy or shrewd politics, as Hebert indicated in his radio report of June 7, 1954. He said:

Apparently we will never learn.

Once again, Washington permitted itself to get pushed into an act of ill-considered diplomacy of the sort that is losing us friends while gaining us nothing.

The five-power military meeting in Washington to consider defense plans for Southeast Asia was a mistake from its inception. Take a look at who was invited to that conference—military leaders from the United States, the host nation, from France, Britain, Australia and New Zealand.

The idea was that these are supposedly the countries with the biggest stake in seeing that the Red aggression is stopped in Southeast Asia.

However, the composition is objectionable to those whom we should be trying to reach; it is exclusively a white man's show, whereas the area concerned is at least ninety-five per cent yellow and brown.

None of these five nations, actually, is considered an Asian nation in the generally accepted sense of that term. . . .[59]

Not only did Hebert see American policies faltering because of an apparent misunderstanding of the true nature of the conflict in Indo-China, but he also saw the Geneva Conference, whose only real accomplishment was the partition of Vietnam, as a complete failure in maintaining the peace of the future.

The Geneva Conference failed miserably to work out any solution. It failed to accomplish anything, as is now apparent. But the problem cannot be overlooked. Some way must be found to prevent the probable loss of Vietnam from leading to the loss of the rest of the peninsula.[60]

A comment by Mr. Hebert concerning the Geneva talks of 1954 was equally applicable to the Paris peace talks of 1968–1969. On May 25, 1954, the Congressman said:

Isn't it perfectly obvious that the communists want delay [in the peace talks] in order to gain military victory there [Indo-China].[61]

On the War in Vietnam

From 1954 to 1959 the war in Vietnam was suspended. In 1959, however, communist guerillas in South Vietnam began the subversion of the government of Ngo Dinh Diem, as well as the Geneva accords of 1954. Consequently, in May, 1960, upon the request of the South Vietnamese government, President Eisenhower increased the number of American advisers from approximately three hundred to approximately seven hundred.

Involvement in the Vietnamese conflict came gradually for Americans. In December, 1961, President Kennedy authorized further military assistance for the Diem government. Then, American troop strength which had risen to about four thousand in 1962, leaped to fifteen thousand in 1963 and to twenty-three thousand by the end of 1964.

In 1965 massive American intervention followed the Gulf of Tonkin incident of August, 1964. A few days after that incident

Congress approved the Southeast Asia resolution (H.J. Res. 1145) and thus the United States became heavily committed to another war in Asia. To quote Mr. Hebert, our nation had been "back-doored" into war.

By 1965, then, the United States was faced with the decision to defend its men and equipment in Vietnam or pull out and permit a communist victory. The Johnson Administration decided to use a large number of American troops in an effort to prevent the communist conquest of South Vietnam. Though this decision was contrary to Hebert's earlier ideas of "Vietnamizing" the war, he, nevertheless, realized the magnitude of the communist threat and voted for the Tonkin resolution.

Once the United States was committed to action in Vietnam, Mr. Hebert came to the support of President Johnson's decision on involvement. He said:

> I've backed the policy of the President because I think he is right. I sympathize with his agony of decision.[62]

Indeed, once the United States commitment was made to the South Vietnamese, the old streak of war-time realism reappeared in Hebert's thinking. As with so many other Americans, Hebert believes that when a nation commits itself to fighting a war, it must also commit itself to fighting for victory. There were those persons who disagreed with the idea of an American commitment in Vietnam and this division of opinion gave rise to the terms "hawk" to describe one who favored the commitment, and "dove" to describe those who, in some way, opposed the commitment.

In his usual forthright manner, Hebert made his position known from the beginning of the controversy. He told his colleagues that

> I am not ashamed to be addressed as a 'hawk.' I want to be a hawk because I want to win, and I want to get those boys back here.[63]

This did not mean, however, that Hebert was to agree with the Johnson Administration on the conduct of the war. When Secretary of Defense Robert McNamara asked Mr. Hebert for his thoughts relating to the conduct of the war, the Congressman replied unhesitatingly that the United States should send four million troops to Vietnam if that number would hurry the day of victory and peace. He added that the United States should be prepared to spend tremendous treasure if that would contribute to a speedy victory and an end to dying. Finally, the Congressman said, with regard to whether or not he favored the bombing of North Vietnam:

> Emphatically, yes! It seems ridiculous to me to just bomb for the sake of bombing limited targets. Now I don't mean to go into North Vietnam and bomb out Hanoi, or bomb out the people of Haiphong. . . . We must hit and destroy anything that contributes to the killing of our people.[64]

A sharp difference of opinion regarding the war soon became apparent in the thinking of the Congressman as opposed to the policies being followed by the Johnson Administration. The Administration continued to work for a political settlement evolving from a limited military operation. For the communists, that policy had the disadvantage of being interpreted as a fundamental weakness. In the communist world of the twentieth century, decisions and events remain black and white, there are no greys—one wins or loses, one is victorious or defeated. Idealism is a rare commodity in the front ranks of a communist army. Mr. Hebert constantly expressed his hope that the Administration would take firm measures to achieve a military victory. On one occasion he said:

> It is my hope . . . that the Administration will go full out to win in Vietnam. This it has not done up to this time.
> I have told Mr. McNamara, personally, that we cannot fight in Vietnam with one arm tied behind our back. It is my conviction, a very strong conviction, that war is a dirty business. You either kill or be killed. I don't believe that there are any niceties in war. . . . We have to bring the enemy to heel as quickly as we can. Up to this moment this has not been done. We have spared them in many instances when we should have not spared them. I believe we should destroy, bomb, and take out everything in North Vietnam that contributes to the killing of one American soldier. . . . It is something I feel very keenly about, it is something that I have very definite feelings about! [65]

A military victory, however, was not to be the course set by the Administration, and Hebert was quick to perceive that America would be engaging in the same frustrating gyrations that had accompanied American involvement in the Korean conflict. Clearly, the Administration's course was not Hebert's approach, and he told his constituents:

> There can be no mistake regarding my position [on the war in Vietnam], I'm the hawkish hawk of all the hawks. I want to get out of Vietnam as quickly as possible, but I don't want to get out with anything less than a victory. Now, again, we hear these remarks about honorable peace, honorable negotiations. Who amongst us wants anything dishonorable, whether he be dove or whether he be hawk.[66]

A short time later the Congressman re-emphasized his basic disagreement with the conduct of the war. He said:

> I'm a hawk. I disagree with the progress of the war. It hasn't been fast enough for me. I want to win and get out.[67]

The reasoning upon which Mr. Hebert's position was founded was sharp and to the point. He explained:

> I think it's academic to discuss why we're there [Vietnam], the fact is we are there and we can't afford to lose. . . . we can't run . . . we can't pick up our tent and slip away. We have to win.[68]

Why must the United States win? Why is it that this nation cannot afford to lose? Mr. Hebert explained further:

> This is a fight . . . for us to keep the Communists away from our shores. This is what we're fighting for.[69]

Then, in the late 1960's, especially during the various political campaigns of 1968, the merits of the Administration's policy of continuing the American presence in Vietnam was loudly debated. When questioned concerning his opinion of the Administration's policy in Vietnam, Mr. Hebert responded:

> This is no time for disunity. Disagree with the President [Johnson] on his domestic policy, but let's uphold his hand, and uphold it strongly, as high as that hand in New York harbor.[70]

As criticism of Johnson's Vietnam policy mounted, and the suggestion was put forth that undue criticism only aided the enemy by leading him to believe that American public opinion was somewhat less than certain regarding its commitment to freedom, Hebert said:

> Now, there is no need of me telling you again that I disagree with the President [Johnson] in his domestic policies. I think my record shows that I vehemently and vigorously disagree with so many of his domestic programs which I think are leading us down the road to statism, socialism, and give-aways. But in the international field, I cannot agree with him more heartily, or share in his concern more vigorously.[71]

In 1968, the belligerents in Vietnam agreed to hold peace talks in Paris. For those who could remember, the Paris talks soon became reminiscent of the Geneva conference of 1954 in that there was a complete lack of any desire on the communist side for a meaningful peace settlement in Vietnam.

Two years before these talks began, Secretary McNamara asked Mr. Hebert his opinion on putting out peace feelers to Hanoi. In reporting his reply to Mr. McNamara's query, Hebert told his constituents:

> As to peace feelers, I told the Secretary, 'Put out your peace feelers, but they are not going to amount to a tinker's dam.' But you must put them out. You must do it. And what have we done? We put out the peace feelers and they have failed as I said they would fail. . . . We come now to the conclusion. What must we do? We must . . . win . . . and unless we win, we have a dismal future ahead.[72]

Thus, with the vantage of hindsight into the fiascoes of Korea and Vietnam, a conclusion that every American must sooner or later arrive at, is the sobering thought expressed by the Congressman.

> After Vietnam, we must think twice before we start sending American boys to foreign soil to defend a foreign country.[73]

CHAPTER IV

POLITICS, PARTIES AND POLITICIANS

U<small>NTIL RECENTLY IN</small> our country's history, whenever someone mentioned the word "politics," he was usually referring to the local political organization or, at best, the quadrennial occupants of the state capitol. Today, however, whenever politics is mentioned, the speaker is usually speaking within the context of national politics, and, in all probability, his remarks concern the presidency. In a democracy such as ours, it is only proper that all levels of government should fall under the scrutiny of the American people. Thus Congress is a focal point of national attention. Again, this is only proper because Congress bears the responsibility of representing the political mood of America. F. Edward Hebert is keenly aware of the function and responsibilities of our national legislature and its membership.

On Congress

Since school days, Congressman Hebert has had a deep respect for Congress. His appreciation of the functions of our national lawmaking body and the opportunities it affords the representatives of the people remains today as solidly fixed as when, as a freshman congressman, he said:

> This national congress is a great institution. There one sees all races, all creeds, all nationalities, all types of political thought and theory. It is a great melting pot of cross-country ideas and expressions; a vast proving ground for new ideas and new thoughts in government; a gigantic platform from which is expressed the

views of every section of the country—a forum where freedom of speech and freedom of the press are supreme. There is no hamper on speech. A member of Congress may say what he thinks and what he likes and there is no one to gag him. The youngest members have as much right on the floor as the oldest members. The lowest ranking member is given equal privileges with the Speaker and the majority and minority leaders. There is no censorship of the *Congressional Record*. It is the freest press in all the world.[1]

In the thirty years since his first election to Congress in November, 1940, Mr. Hebert has remained acutely conscious of the fact that he is first and foremost the representative of Louisiana's First Congressional District. Six months after first taking his seat in Congress, Hebert said:

> I became the spokesman in Washington on the floor of Congress for every man, woman and child irrespective of race, color or creed who resides in the First Congressional District of Louisiana, and as such I come before you tonight to make an accounting of my stewardship. . . .
> My election to Congress did not mean to me that I was given a blanket order to go to Washington to do as I liked regardless of the views, opinions and desires of the people of my district. My election as your Congressman merely meant that you were selecting me to go to Washington to express your views and to cast my vote in accordance with your wishes and your preferences.[2]

Thus, Hebert occupies a seat in the House of Representatives in order to reflect the majority opinion of his constituents—a purpose that has never eluded him. Shortly after completing his first term in Congress, Hebert told a luncheon meeting of the Young Men's Business Club:

> As I told Sam Rayburn one day when somebody was discussing the idea that Congress should lead the people, I emphatically disagreed with him, and I think properly so. I don't think your representatives in Congress should attempt to lead you. They should follow you. Your representative is there to express your wishes. As I told the Speaker, if more of us Democrats in the 77th Con-

gress had followed our people instead of trying to lead them and tell them what to do, there wouldn't be so few of us back there today. . . .

We are your representatives doing what you want. If the people don't want certain things, no one man is big enough to tell them they have got to have them, and you will have that kind of government just so long as you protect your own interests—but the day that you become lackadaisical, you falter and fall by the wayside, that is when that minority will gain control of the country, and if they do, God help us all! [3]

More than ten years later Mr. Hebert re-emphasized the representative character of Congress and presented some additional thoughts. He said:

The House and Senate number 531 men and women. Congress represents a good cross section of human nature. . . .

In Congress we have doctors, lawyers, newspaper publishers, farmers, and others from all walks of life and endeavor.

As a group Congress reflects the faults, the whims, the failings of the American people.

Congress is Americana.

The voters sent these men and women to Washington to speak for them. The voters 'hired' these people, so to speak, to represent them in the world's greatest legislative body.

The voter is the common denominator in the crazy-quilt pattern of personalities that is Congress.

But some of the people's elected representatives take their job lightly. Some lack the courage and strength of character to stand up for the demands of the voters in their home districts. They exploit their position in the governmental system to advance their own private interests.

Others are beholding to special interest groups, such as labor unions. Another group serves as Charlie McCarthy for a particular segment of industry—seeking only what is good for their particular special interest—and falling down on the job they were hired to do by the people in their home districts. . . .

The more nearly the members of Congress represent the people, the closer the government is to the people. The people, after all, are the employers of those of us who sit in the halls of Congress.[4]

Hebert is of the opinion that responsibility in a democracy is a two-way street. The representatives of the people certainly have a definite responsibility to those they represent. On the other hand, the citizen in a democratic nation must shoulder a heavy responsibility. The Congressman has described the citizen's responsibility in the following terms.

A man cannot get to Congress unless he is elected by the people, and if Congress is lax in its responsibility, then charge the error to the people who elected the undesirable members of Congress. It is within the power of the people, if they will only exercise that power, to turn out any and all members of Congress who do not represent their constituency properly; that is the reason a member of the House must give an accounting of his stewardship every two years; that is the reason why a member of the House of Representatives can only acquire his seat by direct election of the people; that is the reason that the method of selecting the members of the House of Representatives alone has not changed since the Constitution was written.

More guilty than anyone else for what we have in government today are the majority of qualified voters in America who failed to exercise their right of ballot in the last presidential election [1948]. It is shocking to record that in this republic the people did not take the time, or have interest enough in the welfare of their nation, to vote in the last presidential election. They slept on their rights and cannot blame anyone else for what is happening today in this country. That majority who stayed away from the polls is guilty of contributory negligence to the crime of poor citizenship.[5]

Confirmed in his belief that a Congressman should represent his constituency to the best of his ability, Mr. Hebert is equally convinced of the merits of the two-year term of office for members of the House of Representatives. The following excerpt tells why.

I have heard it asked often: Wouldn't it be better if a Member of the House was elected for more than two years? That would be a most cruel blow against our democracy.... Against our form of government.... That is your safeguard that the government still belongs to you and you can control it.

Your House of Representatives is your sounding board, and the day those representatives up there don't do what you want them to do, you not only should, but it is your duty to remove them from office. That is the reason why every two years you have an opportunity to express your opinion. You don't have to wait, you don't have to wait four, six, eight, or ten years.[6]

In still another political realm, one that is frequently in the spotlight of events, the relationship between the executive and legislative branches of our government, Mr. Hebert has maintained the opinion that there should always be a spirit of cooperation existing between the two branches of government. Often, however, the executive branch tends to overlook Congress in arriving at important national decisions. A case in point was the decision of the Department of Defense to close certain military bases around the country in 1964 and 1965. Mr. Hebert was questioned about the relationship between the executive and legislative branches by Ann Corrick on *Washington Viewpoint*, for August 23, 1965. The Congressman used that opportunity to frankly discuss the frequently absent spirit of cooperation between the two branches of government. In part, the dialogue was:

CORRICK: Congressman Hebert, isn't it true that in this nuclear age many of our military bases *are* obsolete, and they *are not* really serving a useful purpose in our overall defense establishment and they should be closed or consolidated?

HEBERT: Nobody can dispute that, but I'll change one word of 'many' to "some." Some are, yes, obsolete, and some are not to be used, but some that have been ordered closed should not have been closed, in my opinion. How can Congress find out what is going on, how can it discharge its responsibility, unless we know the facts?

CORRICK: Well, Congress has a great deal of influence with the executive department. Why don't you demand the facts from the Defense Department?

HEBERT: Well Ann, that is a statement not based on foundation of fact or reality. We are supposed to have the influence which we do not have as exhibited before. It is because this influence has not been recognized. . . . I don't like it. I don't like it a bit, but we're not given these facts, because we're not told these things. Mr. McNamara doesn't confer with us, he tells us what his decision is. Now, we want to know ahead of time what these decisions are so we can be a partner in the dealing. If this was true, if we were taken into a full partnership, well. . . . I may say we're being taken in more and more every day, in every way. The message is getting through apparently, the readings are coming off the computers over in the Pentagon that we will insist upon exercising our prerogatives.[7]

What Mr. Hebert emphasized in 1965, what many of his colleagues came to recognize and act upon some years later, is that Congress controls the purse strings, and they want to know that the nation's finances are being conscientiously dispended by the executive department of government.

On Legislation

As every American schoolboy knows, each branch of the government has its special function to perform. The primary function of the legislative branch is to enact necessary legislation for the country. A proposed piece of legislation, however, can be removed from the legislative process, without any discussion of the bill's merits, through a parliamentary maneuver by one opposed to the bill. Obstructionist tactics such as these have prompted Mr. Hebert to maintain, throughout his career, that regardless of the merits of a bill, it should be given a fair hearing. Thus, shortly after his first election to Congress, he said:

I believe all legislation should be considered by the House and not killed off through a parliamentary maneuver.[8]

On the other hand, Mr. Hebert has never regarded legislation as being permanent. He is keenly aware of the constant changes occurring in American society and recognizes that what was thought to be a good law or a necessary law in the past may not be a good or necessary law in the present. In this connection, he has said:

> In a dynamic society such as ours, the laws must be revised and improved to keep pace with the changing times. Weak laws should be repealed or amended to conform to popular demand.[9]

This view he later reaffirmed when he said:

> No law is perfect; as the years pass, and conditions change, revisions and amendments to the laws become necessary. The statute books must and should be kept up to date. If something in the law is harmful, then it must be reviewed and re-written to make it fair to all. But even a good law cannot accomplish its purpose unless it is administered in fairness and justice.[10]

On Congressional Investigations

One method by which Congress determines the merits of proposed legislation is through the work of its committees. The committees, in turn, usually rely upon informed people throughout the land to voice their opinion, to offer testimony, or to demonstrate their expertise in favor of or in opposition to a proposed piece of legislation. Some congressional committees perform the valuable and necessary services of conducting investigations into certain problems within American society. Legislation, in such an instance, may be the end product rather than the motivating factor of these congressional hearings. In any case, congressional committee investigations can, and usually do, generate considerable controversy. Such controversy, Hebert believes, can be held within the bounds of propriety only if the chairman of the committee understands his responsibilities. The Congressman has said:

> I think I must say in complete candor that the dignity and decorum, the dispatch and the demeanor of persons at a hearing, are in every instance but the length and shadow of the judgment and discretion, the restraint and the capacity of the chairman and the committee conducting the inquiry. No law and few rules can cope with every human quirk. But the healthy and wholesome use

of the gavel by the chairman can enforce the rules and can keep the hearing within the bounds of propriety, good conduct and public decency. And that can be done without doing violence either to the principle of open and fair dealings or full and frank discussion.[11]

One important point of debate is usually built upon the procedures of the committee in the fear that these may compromise the personal rights of witnesses. Mr. Hebert's position is founded upon a strict ethic which is best explained in the following excerpt.

I believe that before any testimony is taken in public in controversial issues which might involve the good name or reputation of an individual, the committee itself should be cognizant of what testimony is to be offered. If an accusation is to be made against an individual, that individual should have the right and the privilege of denying the accusation under the protection of an executive session of the committee. If the accused makes a flat denial of the charges and there is no other substantiating evidence except the mere assertion or accusation of the accuser, then I do not believe the charges should be given public emphasis. In such instances I most certainly would subscribe to the policy that it is better for ninety-nine guilty to escape than one innocent man be hanged.[12]

During the early 1950's, the era of congressional investigations that included the McCarthy hearings, Mr. Hebert told his constituents:

There may be one constructive result from all these hearings. We may get a working code for Congressional hearings. . . .

[It] is entirely correct that Congress must see to it that its committee procedures are proper and fair. . . .

To continue to hold the respect and support of the American people, Congressional committees must have firm and fair rules of conduct. . . .

The greatest tool for good government Congress has is its investigating authority. It shouldn't abuse it.[13]

Furthermore, Mr. Hebert has consistently supported the idea that

A committee should achieve the prestige and respect from the American people as a whole that such a group must command if it is to do its job completely.[14]

Hence, at no time in his career has Hebert ever had kind words for anyone or any political party that would use an investigating committee of Congress for any purpose other than the good of the nation. During the course of the many investigations of the 1950's, Mr. Hebert said:

> There seems to be a trend these days. Most of the political news in recent months has developed from radio and television programs or from congressional hearings that have been staged for radio, television and the newsreels. Unfortunately, most of the Capitol Hill investigations in the last few years have been designed for the klieg lights.
>
> The newsmen and cameramen have contributed in great part to all of the whoop-la surrounding congressional hearings. They build the event up in advance, then howl that freedom of the press is being violated if the committees try to bar them.[15]

Expressing similar thoughts a year later, Mr. Hebert said:

> There have been . . . certain practices which, in my view, are to be condemned. I do not believe it is a contribution to the public good to turn a hearing of the Congress into a stage performance with the actors preening themselves before the camera; and with the viewers taking over the conduct of the proceedings. The information elicited at these hearings is for other purposes than entertainment. That type of hearing gets itself into the position where the reproduction of the hearing becomes more important than the subject under inquiry.[16]

Indeed, for a long time Congressman Hebert has opposed televising congressional hearings. His opposition has nothing to do with censorship but rather is based upon the effect that television has on the participants in the hearing. He has written:

> I ruled out TV when I first became Chairman of the Investigating Committee almost eight years ago, long before Speaker Rayburn's ruling. I had a great deal of experience with televised

hearings, particularly during my membership on the Committee on Un-American Activities. That was the first time a Congressional hearing was televised. I believe the glaring klieg lights and microphones place the witness at a distinct disadvantage. On the other side of the table, I believe it stimulates members of Congress to become ham actors instead of legislators.

Of course I agree that the public has a right to know what goes on in these hearings, and they do have their representatives there in both members of the press and radio. . . .[17]

Senator Joseph McCarthy was the subject of a report by Hebert to his constituents. In April, 1950, the Congressman said, subsequent to Senator McCarthy's charges of communism in the State Department:

I do not subscribe nor do I agree with what Senator McCarthy is saying or the manner in which he is pursuing the subject. . . .[18]

Four years later Senator McCarthy shared the spotlight of Mr. Hebert's criticism with the noted news commentator Edward R. Murrow. Explaining the controversy then raging between the Senator and Mr. Murrow over the Civil Liberties Union, Mr. Hebert pointed out that to a degree both men were correct in their statements. But, he indicated, there was more involved in the issue than simply their statements. Deflecting the flak of the antagonists' verbal barrage, Hebert discovered partisan politics to be in the background of the entire squabble. He said:

The exchange between Senator McCarthy and Mr. Murrow is important in that it follows the pattern of partisans not only involved in the controversy over McCarthyism but also in political controversies between Republican and Democratic parties. Neither party is without sin. Both are equally guilty in their attempt to make the general public believe that their cause is right when in reality their main objective is control by their respective parties and what is good for the nation as a whole is only their secondary objective.[19]

A few years before the above statement was made, Mr. Hebert had addressed himself squarely to the issue of partisan politics entering into congressional hearings. In a letter to former Governor Thomas E. Dewey of New York, the Congressman wrote:

> While I am a Democrat I do not regard the activities and the investigations of the committee [House Un-American Activities Committee] as being either Republican or Democrat. It is my contention and belief that the objective of these investigations should rise above partisan politics, and should never at any time fall below the level of national security.[20]

One aspect of congressional investigations that has greatly concerned Mr. Hebert is the methods of gathering evidence. Speaking on this subject, he has said:

> The Constitution does provide rigid safeguards against abuse of individual rights in detecting suspects. . . .
>
> Modern electronics has given us another means of crime detection, by wiretapping. It follows that similar safeguards should prevail against the use of indiscriminate monitoring. . . .
>
> When the security of the United States and the liberties of all of us are at stake, wiretapping is justified. But in the case of ordinary crimes, Congress should think twice before legalizing such a procedure. . . .
>
> If Federal agents are given unlimited authority to wiretap, great holes will be ripped in the fabric of the American concept of freedom and law.
>
> America must be protected from its internal enemies but in so doing, the freedoms which we are trying to protect must not be destroyed, less we destroy all freedom.[21]

The Congressman has not been found solely in the posture of critic. On the contrary, he is one among that rare breed of men who actively work to rectify abuses whenever they occur. In March, 1954, he said:

> My desire to become a member of the Committee on Un-American Activities was motivated by a desire to change the manner in which the investigations were being conducted at the time and to which I did not agree. My insistence that anybody named or charged at a public hearing by a witness should be given equal opportunity to appear before the same forum at the earliest pos-

sible time following his request to appear, I believe, was an important contribution to the proceedings.[22]

While serving on the Un-American Activities Committee, Mr. Hebert described the work of those who would subvert our constitutional government. He said:

> Cleverly, adroitly, cunningly, there are those who are tireless in their efforts to lead away from our fundamental ideals of freedom and our imbedded American way of life. They have gone, are going and will go, to any extreme to accomplish their set purpose.[23]

The Congressman is acutely aware of the fact, however, that the tactics used in rooting out enemies of democracy can become dangerously akin to the operations of the enemy himself. Mr. Hebert has said:

> The great danger in fighting a totalitarian state—whether it is fascistic or communistic—is that we adopt, or are liable to adopt, the very same methods and thought controls that we are fighting.
>
> That can't happen to us in our fight against communism. We cannot sacrifice our freedom and the rights of individuals to fight communism because we don't need to do so. We are strong enough, and are powerful enough to fight communism with American methods.
>
> The methods which are embedded in our Constitution, the right of trial by jury, the right to face the accuser—all of these things and many more must be preserved if we are to keep this nation the great free nation we have come to love and honor.[24]

Furthermore, Mr. Hebert is firmly convinced that the hearings of the Internal Security Committee of the House of Representatives must always remain non-partisan. To this end he has said:

> As far as I am personally concerned, I don't regard the hearings as Republican or Democrat, I look on them . . . as American. The most important thing is the security of this country, and I don't care whether it is a Republican or a Democrat, if any individual is guilty of espionage, any individual is guilty of disloyalty to his

country, he should be brought out into the open, whether he is Republican or Democrat.[25]

An issue often debated before the Internal Security Committee is whether or not the Communist party of the United States should be outlawed. Mr. Hebert's position on this question is based upon the soundest logic. The essence of his thinking is found in the following excerpt.

> I am opposed to outlawing the Communist party [in the United States] because to do so is to drive them underground and it thus becomes more difficult to detect them. . . . To drive the Communist party underground is to weaken our offensive against them. I feel very strongly that the Communists should be allowed to speak as much as they want to speak because the day that we become afraid to allow a Communist to get up on a soap box and say what he wants to say, that is the day that we deny to him that which we are fighting for.[26]

In the final analysis, Mr. Hebert finds that

> With all its faults, with all its errors of omission and commission, the Un-American Activities Committee of the House of Representatives has done a noble job in the interest of American security.[27]

Indeed, the Congressman has always been the advocate of fair and impartial hearing by Congressional committees, whether they involve friend or foe, virtue or vice, for without fair play and impartial treatment, the committees' reports can result in legislation detrimental to American society. He has concluded that

> The worst laws are those enacted in defiance, haste, or fear.[28]

On Objectivity from the Mass Media

There must also be a sense of fair play in reporting the work of Congress. Over the years Mr. Hebert has repeatedly stated the obligation of the reporter to be as objective in his work as is humanly possible. There are few men in Congress better qualified to lecture the fourth estate. Mr. Hebert has said:

It was because of my newspaper work that I was literally cata-pulted into the Congress of the United States. Six months before I was elected I had no ambitions to rise to the top of my lifelong profession—the newspaper game. I never intended my newspaper work to be a stepping stone to political office—elective or other-wise. . . . I make this statement because while a member of Con-gress I have never forgotten that I really am a newspaperman and [that I am] most jealous of the heritage and traditions of news-papers and their reporters.[29]

The impact of Hebert's newspaper career has clearly revealed itself during his Congressional career. This is discerned in the fol-lowing comment.

It is . . . years since I have struck the keys of a typewriter to earn my living but I have never ceased being at heart the reporter which I started out to be.

I still think like a reporter. I still reason like a reporter. I still like to think of myself as a reporter.[30]

The fact that Mr. Hebert was a newspaper reporter and editor for over twenty years before going to Congress has also affected his approach to getting all the facts before reporting an event. He has said:

Never forgetting my background and my profession, I natu-rally, perhaps, am affected more by sloppy, inaccurate or deliber-ately untrue reporting than other members of Congress but the ultimate effect on them is just as damaging and lasting as it is on me.[31]

In addition, the Congressman has spoken on the consequences of accurate reporting:

As a former newspaper reporter I have always been alert and sensitive to reporting the news accurately in order that those who read and depend on the newspapers might have the full knowl-edge of what is factually the case.[32]

From this background, then, there is no difficulty in under-standing the Congressman's position when it comes to inaccurate reporting or baseless charges of censorship from the news media.

He has been a consistent fighter against both abuses. Early in his career Hebert told his colleagues:

> Once again I am compelled to avail myself of the privileges extended a member of the Congress to direct attention . . . to a certain segment of the press, which, from its editorial pages and news columns, screams for the freedom of the press, and yet, muffles the voices of those who seek to exercise and perpetuate freedom of expression.
>
> The time has come, Mr. Speaker, when the masks of hypocrisy should be torn from the faces of these journalistic Jekyll and Hydes and their perfidy exposed in all its ugly nakedness.
>
> Those of us who love freedom of expression, whether it be on the printed pages of newspapers, through the microphones of the radio or from the public platform, must accept as our responsibility the task of exposing these journalistic harlots and charlatans, lest through their sabotage from within, they destroy that freedom of expression upon which this nation is builded.
>
> Not only, Mr. Speaker, is 'Eternal vigilance the price of liberty' but eternal vigilance should be the watchword of America in zealously guarding freedom of expression and ever keeping on the alert for the mouthings of those who would march under the valiant banner of such a freedom and yet deny that same freedom to those who do not possess the same or an equal medium of expression as they.
>
> Remember that as long as freedom of expression lives in this country, America lives. When freedom of expression dies, America dies.
>
> There are some editors and news purveyors in this country who preach freedom of speech but practice it not when it involves them or conflicts with their views.
>
> These narrow-minded, bigoted men . . . gnaw away at the very foundation of our form of government by reckless charges, false and untrue, without fear of correction or repudiation because they refuse to give to those so attacked and maligned the right to answer and defend themselves through the same medium by which they are attacked.
>
> It is not my purpose, Mr. Speaker, in making these remarks to even suggest that I would attempt to stay the hand which pens

such calumnies. Indeed not. On the contrary, I defend their right to write and speak as they so desire. It is their right under the freedom of expression, which I champion, to write and say what they please. But, by the Eternal, Mr. Speaker, I declare that it is equally the right of the attacked to face his accuser on a common meeting ground and to let the people determine for themselves which is right and which is wrong. Could anybody ask for less?

I regard the newspapers and radio of this country as much responsible to the people of this nation as any elected official who holds office through the sufferance of the electorate. As you well know, I am a newspaperman by profession and I am proud of that profession, and because I have always accepted it as a public trust, responsible to the people who are the bone and sinew of this nation and who accord me the freedom of expression which I enjoy, that I resent most bitterly any action or practice which would tend to destroy that privilege.[33]

Mr. Hebert is also quite articulate with regard to the disadvantage that a Congressman faces in getting his side of the story over to the public as opposed to the reporter or newscaster who can reach a multitude of listeners or readers in a short space of time. In an open letter to newspaper reporters and radio commentators, he said:

> Members of Congress are at a distinct disadvantage in presenting their views and opinions to their constituency and to the American public. They are literally in the hands of the newspaper reporter and the radio commentator. The newspaper reporter, through the newspapers of the country, has a potential field of millions of readers. The radio commentator, in my opinion, has an even greater field because, since the advent of the radio, millions of men and women depend on the radio newscast and the expressions of individual commentators for their main source of news and information.
>
> Members of Congress, on the contrary, have a limited audience which, in comparison to the field covered by the newspapers and radios, is most insignificant. A member of Congress, for the better part, addresses sparsely filled galleries and has only the limited circulation of the *Congressional Record* for complete quotes.
>
> A newspaper reporter, or radio news commentator, holds the

life and death decision over what he will report to the nation concerning Congress. His judgment is final. His interpretation of what is news is what reaches the general public. His opinion of the value of what a Member of Congress says on the floor is what the American public receives and not, in all too many cases, of what a Member of Congress actually says or does, or what in the final analysis, is really the important thing. The reporter is constantly on the alert for the punch lines which will make the headlines.

It is easy to understand, therefore, the great responsibility which is charged the press and radio of America.

America has a free press. Its only restraint, and that only during war time, is a voluntary censorship. Pray God that the free press in America will continue because when a free press dies, democracy dies. I am naturally a champion of a free press being what I am, and I believe it to be not only the right, but the duty, of a free press to criticize.

If the new Congress [78th] has an opportunity, an opportunity expressed by Mr. Clapper as 'second only to that which was given to the forefathers,' then I submit that the press and radio of America have an equal opportunity of demonstrating to the men and women of America their right to continue as a free and unbridled press and radio.

If honesty, sincerity of purpose, and devotion to country is asked of every citizen, certainly it is not asking too much of the press and radio of America in these trying times to exhibit the same honesty, the same sincerity of purpose, and the same devotion to country as demanded and expected of every other individual.[34]

Mr. Hebert is a staunch advocate of freedom and responsibility in all aspects of American life. For this reason he could write:

I believe that the tendency of too many newspapers in this country is to grind axes for selfish interests instead of engaging in the fair and impartial dissemination of news. I believe, of course, in the freedom of the press and I would never advocate anything which would curtail or reflect that freedom, but I believe that the press in general should recognize its own great responsibility and protect that freedom by not abusing its power.[35]

Concerning the freedom of the press, Mr. Hebert has written:

> When my service in Congress is ended, I hope to be able to get
> a job on a newspaper again, but I'll be damned if I want to go back
> to work on a press which is not as free and unshackled as the day
> I left it.[36]

On Party Fealty

Perhaps it is this sense of fair play or perhaps it is that restless
individualism that has led Hebert to the ever-present and decidedly
strong attitude he maintains with regard to partisan politics. This
attitude has been expressed in a number of statements over the
years of his political career.

Quite early in that career, after being attacked for not allowing
himself to be pushed along by prevailing political winds, Mr. Hebert began to utter his thoughts about the responsibility and integrity of the legislator that have cast him as a paragon of political
independence in the House of Representatives. In 1945 he said:

> My appreciation of my office is to vote in accordance with the
> views of the majority of my district which may or may not neces-
> sarily be my own personal view.[37]

Furthermore,

> I shall reserve at all times the right to support and cast my ballot
> and raise my voice for those candidates and those individuals who
> have my preference for public office.[38]

And,

> I have exercised the right which I champion for any man—the
> right to support and vote for those candidates, in whose judgment
> he considers the best interests of the community we all love will
> be best served.[39]

Thus before a microphone on an evening in 1945, F. Edward
Hebert, the two-term congressman from New Orleans, served
notice on the national Democratic organization and Louisiana
politicians that he was not the tool, the pawn, or the lackey of any
political group. Instead, his service was dedicated to the people of
the First Congressional District.

Indeed, Mr. Hebert has little patience with those politicians who maintain the double standard of support for democratic freedoms and, at the same time, allow themselves to be bridled about by the dictates of party leaders. He has said:

> Those who prate of freedom of speech, freedom of the press, freedom of expression, freedom of every man to cast his vote as his conscience dictates, unmask themselves as hypocrites, expose themselves as traitors to democracy, unveil themselves as deceitful embryonic dictators when they pursue a course of condemnation and attempt to crucify on the heights of a Calvary of public opinion, those who dare exercise their inalienable rights as free men.[40]

During the primary campaign of 1948, Mr. Hebert's opposition gambled that his voting independence might be upsetting to the predominantly Democratic First District. Thus, the opposition made a timid attempt to suggest that Mr. Hebert's voting record could be a campaign issue. Without hesitation, the Congressman picked up the gauntlet saying:

> It has been charged by the opposition that I have voted a majority of times with the Republicans instead of with the Democrats.
>
> I'm glad that observation has been made.
>
> If it is true that I voted more often with the Republicans, it is an example of the fact that I don't care whether legislation is sponsored by Republicans or Democrats. This is not the deciding factor in how I cast my vote. The deciding factor is what legislation is best for America. . . .[41]

A year later, after having openly supported Strom Thurmond in the 1948 presidential campaign (Thurmond was also Louisiana's favorite) and after being the object of considerable criticism for bolting the Democratic candidate, Mr. Hebert spelled out his position once more. He said:

> I was elected as a Democrat and sit as a Democrat through the votes of the people of my district of the sovereign State of Louisiana and I will vote according to their wishes and not under the compulsion of leadership which would destroy the sovereignty

of the State, establish a welfare state, or will I be subject to threats and intimidation of a chief executive who resorts to such practices.[42]

Then, in 1949, he wrote:

I hope I never come to the position when I will vote for or against any legislation just because the administration advocates it. That is exactly what I have been fighting against—judging legislation on a partisan basis. All the saints are not on my team nor are all the sinners on the other side of the aisle.[43]

In April, 1950, Mr. Hebert anounced his candidacy for re-election to Congress and, anticipating that the opposition might peddle as an issue his support for Thurmond in 1948, Hebert issued a statement designed to serve a two-fold purpose. First, it restated his position on non-partisan voting and, secondly, it offered an explanation for his opposition to many of the Truman Administration's legislative proposals. He said:

Because I am a Democrat does not mean that I have to conform to everything the national Democratic Committee subscribes. If I did that I would have to become a traitor to my constituents . . . and a Judas to the concept of government preached by Thomas Jefferson.

What good is a democracy if an elected member of Congress is going to take his orders from a few party bosses in Washington.

If such a procedure is to prevail why have any Congress at all? If your elected representatives are not supposed to make up their own minds then why have elected representatives at all?

I am a Democrat and I will remain a Democrat but being a Democrat does not mean that I will look with awe and cringe when Democratic party chieftains speak. There is nothing to indicate that any political party is infallible nor are they descended from the diety.

A conformist Democrat is a Democrat who does not think for himself, but who allows the party leader to do his thinking for him.

A conformist Democrat is one who takes the instructions of the National Democratic leadership in preference to the wishes of his own people back home whom he is supposed to represent.

A conformist Democrat is the party hack who kids himself into the belief that abject submission and lack of independence is the stamp of party loyalty and the path of recognition and reward.

A nonconformist Democrat is the Democrat who believes in the principles and ideals of the Democratic party as it was founded but who refuses to allow himself to be counted in the bag on all issues just because he is a Democrat.[44]

During the primary campaign that followed, the opposition once again miscalculated when it tried to develop Mr. Hebert's partisan independence into a campaign issue. To the feeble, indeed ridiculous, suggestion that he was a disloyal Democrat, Mr. Hebert retorted:

I definitely will not follow the Democratic party blindly or any other party for that matter. I definitely cannot be relied upon to be a rubber stamp for any party leadership. I will positively not vote on legislation based on whether a Democrat or a Republican proposes it.

Above all, I shall continue to refuse to be stamped as any segment's congressman. I will not be labor's congressman and I will not be management's congressman. I shall continue to vote for the best interests of both labor and management and not favor one over the other.[45]

Three days later, in order to make certain that the above statement was well understood by the opposition, and also in order to prevent the statement from becoming a one-time utterance lost in the welter of campaigning, Mr. Hebert gave new emphasis to his long-established independence. He said:

You know I have always prided myself on my independence and the fact that I can never be accused of being a 'rubber stamp' of the Truman Administration, the Democratic leadership in Congress or anybody else.[46]

This was but the introduction to a hard-hitting speech that strongly re-emphasized the candidate's dedication to independence of action in his Congressional duties.

Following the Congressional elections of November, 1950, Mr.

Hebert told those in attendance at the annual banquet of the staff of Baptist Hospital in New Orleans:

> I do not believe in blind party loyalty. True, I am a Democrat but I like to believe myself as something of a non-conformist Democrat who votes neither Democrat nor Republican, but American.
>
> The yardstick by which I measure is not how many votes is it worth but is it the right or the wrong thing for the preservation of this nation.[47]

As the election campaigns of 1956 approached, a familiar bleating was heard from the opposition concerning the Congressman's relationship with the leadership of the Democratic party. Patience is certainly a virtue of the man, for once again Hebert explained:

> I am a Democrat, but not a slave.
>
> As a Democrat I have reserved my right as a free man to vote my conscience at all times whether that vote involves issues or candidates. As a member of the Democratic party I have not abdicated my right of free will or given license to brainwash my political philosophy. I am a Democrat who has never left the party of our fathers. I am a Democrat who has consistently stood by the recognition of the rights of individuals, and the sovereignty of the several states.[48]

In 1964 the Congressman clearly defined his political philosophy and what he regards as his political responsibilities in a letter to a constituent. He wrote:

> As for my own philosophy, I am a Democrat of the Jeffersonian school and I believe strongly in the principles upon which the Democrat Party was founded but which have been abandoned by many so-called Democrats. If the day comes when either a Republican or a Democrat is to vote in Congress strictly along party lines or because the leadership of either party has so ordained them, there will not be any need for a Congress.
>
> I appreciate my position as being responsible to the district I represent. Whether or not I have fulfilled that job can only be answered in one way—I have been there [representing the First District] for twenty-four years and never had serious opposition

in my life. Two years in the future I will go before the voters again, and as long as they continue me in the Congress and indicate to me what they want me to do, I will do it. I am not interested in the pursuit of national political ambition. I am only interested in reflecting what my constituency wants.[49]

During the 1960's, when party platforms seemingly became confused with passports to Utopia, there were some congressmen who found that they could not, for reasons of their own, support their party's nominee for the presidency. These people, then, supported the candidate of another party. One consequence was that the Democratic party decided to strip these representatives of the seniority which had accrued to them as a result of their years in Congress. There were two cases of representatives being deprived of their seniority in 1964. One of these gentlemen was from South Carolina and the other was from Mississippi. In 1968 a Louisiana congressman decided to support the candidacy of George Wallace for president. The Democratic party responded by stripping the congressman of the little seniority he had accumulated in the two years since being elected to office. Congressman Hebert, the Dean of the Louisiana Delegation, used this opportunity to restate his beliefs with regard to the relationship between the individual congressman and the party leadership. He said:

Anybody who knows me, anybody who knows what I stand for, anybody who knows for what I fought, knows that I am not a conformist Democrat. I have made no secret of that. . . . When the day comes that I will have to come to Congress with a ring in my nose and do what I am told to do or be punished for it, by this insurgent group in the Democratic party in the House, that is the day that I do not deserve to be a member of the House of Representatives and to represent you.[50]

Mr. Hebert's desire for independence of action is but another result of that sense of fair play that has been a part of this man's philosophy throughout his lifetime. It is, furthermore, an open and constant recognition of his responsibility to his constituents. This supplies a reason for Hebert's objectivity in the face of partisan legislation. He has said:

I have never subscribed to the belief that just because a Democrat introduces a bill it is a good bill or just because a Republican introduces a bill it is a bad bill.

I believe that all legislation should stand on its own feet and on its own merits and should be disposed of on a basis of what is right and wrong and not on a basis of whether it is Democratic or Republican sponsored.[51]

During the early years of the Eisenhower Administration, there was something more than the normal amount of name calling among Democrats and Republicans on the Hill. Deploring this horrible waste of energy and talent, Mr. Hebert told a radio audience:

What we need these days is less name-calling and more play-calling—play-calling that will score touchdowns not for any party or political group—but for the nation as a whole.[52]

The partisan politics of the 1950's would barely compare with the partisan activity of the 1960's. As politicians became more and more polarized in opinion, as the good of the nation was frequently sacrificed for personal opinion or party loyalty, Mr. Hebert saw the problem and lashed out at it. He said:

What do we have in this country today? Partisan politics, partisan endeavors, one decrying the other because one is a Republican and the other is a Democrat. Strictly partisan politics on a party line. When the administration in power is Democratic, anything the Republicans suggest is wrong. When the Republicans are in power, and the Democrats suggest something, that is wrong. Both parties are equally guilty. Both parties are with unclean hands. And this is what we are warned against by the father of our country—George Washington.[53]

Perhaps Mr. Hebert's most concise statement relative to the matter of party loyalty was made during a radio address in 1953. At that time he said:

No political party is more important than your country.[54]

On President Truman

Mr. Hebert's unusual attitude toward partisan politics coupled with his philosophy of America first has often led him into unusual situations with the national leadership of his own party. The outstanding episode in this regard was the famous exchange of correspondence with President Truman which, in the final analysis, led to a tremendous groundswell of popular support for the Congressman's position.

In the dark days of December, 1950, when military events in Korea were reversing the almost certain success of American forces, Hebert suggested to the President:

> Now is the time for our people to set aside whatever differences of opinion that might exist in a unified effort for ultimate success in our fight to continue the freedom of the free peoples of the world. I believe and suggest that the spiritual leaders of our nations be called upon to set aside a Sunday on which the respective pastors shall urge the people of this country to join in prayer to the God of their belief to give to our responsible officials, political and military, the wisdom and the courage, to arrive at the right and proper decisions.[55]

In a terse reply President Truman dismissed Mr. Hebert's suggestion in one sentence, and then wrote:

> I am extremely sorry that the sentiments expressed in your letter were not thought of before November seventh, when the campaign in your State, Utah, North Carolina, Illinois and Indiana was carried on in a manner that was as low as I've ever seen and I've been in this game since 1906.[56]

Once the substance of both letters was made public, popular opinion rushed to the side of Congressman Hebert and his office was deluged with mail supporting his position.*

By the summer of 1952 Hebert's opposition to the Fair Deal had reached the point of near totality. He addressed his constituents saying:

> Yes I am opposed to Truman. . . . Yes I am opposed to the present Democratic Administration; yes, I am opposed to the

---

* The letters of Congressman Hebert and President Truman, along with excerpts from letters to Mr. Hebert concerning this episode, will be found beginning on page 179.

coddling of communism in our government; yes I am opposed to
the destruction of the sovereignty of the individual states; yes, I
am opposed to exploitation of human beings under the guise of
security; yes, I am opposed to any foreign commitments or alli-
ances which do not have as their primary motive the best interests
of America and its people.[57]

Was there a just cause for Hebert's opposition to the policies of
the Truman Administration? There was and the factors contrib-
uting to this cause played a similar and most important role in Hebert's opposition to much of the domestic legislation proposed by
the Kennedy and Johnson administrations. The Congressman's ire
with the Truman Administration was perhaps best expressed in a
radio talk delivered just one month after the first inauguration of
Dwight Eisenhower. Reviewing the results of the Truman years,
Hebert declared:

> The country at the moment is plagued with debt, oppressive
> taxes, a monstruous spending program, undeclared war, prac-
> tically unlimited military commitments abroad and by all the
> vexations attendant upon the previous administration's misrule.[58]

The reason for Mr. Hebert's conclusion was not difficult to find.
By 1953 the policies of the Truman Administration had entered
upon the pages of history, but Mr. Hebert had viewed the socialistic trend of that administration with alarm, particularly after the
President's victory in 1948. To those who regarded the Truman
victory over Dewey as an overwhelming mandate from the American people for a continuation of the policies of Truman's first
term, Hebert said:

> I disagree, however, that Mr. Truman's personal victory was a
> mandate from the people of America to abandon the system
> which has been an inspiration and the incentive for the building
> of the greatest nation which has ever existed.
> Mr. Truman did not receive a majority of the votes of the
> American people. . . . He was the first president in thirty-two
> years to be elected as a minority president. So where does this
> mandate come from to take this nation down the road to so-
> cialism and collectivism.[59]

A short time later the Congressman noted:

The danger and the unmistakable trend in the thinking—the planning—and the actions—of high placed officials can leave no doubt in the minds of even the most casual observer—that each day is bringing us closer to government of men instead of law.[60]

Indeed, Mr. Hebert observed the apparent trend in Administration tactics, spend and spend and elect and elect. Thus, one evening, in a radio broadcast, he said:

The present administration has used the plea of 'gimme' government to get votes. Everything in the land has been promised for nothing.[61]

Aware of such circumstances, Hebert added sometime later:

I would rather have your respect than your vote. That is why from the floor of the House, I denounced the threat of President Truman to either bribe or threaten members of Congress in connection with their votes on the pending labor-management legislation [concerning repeal of Taft-Hartley Labor Relations Act.] [62]

By 1951 Mr. Hebert could discern a growing lack of confidence in the Truman program among his colleagues. He noted, furthermore, that although no formal coalition between Republicans and Southern Democrats had been formed, they had, nevertheless, joined hands to defeat much of the President's program. He was of the opinion that the coalition, despite its loose organization, was an indication that Americans in large numbers were becoming disenchanted with the Truman Administration.[63]

Probably one of the best known events of 1951 was the dismissal of General Douglas MacArthur by President Truman acting in his capacity of commander-in-chief. The incident points up Hebert's complete understanding of the difference between the office of President of the United States and the party leader who happens to occupy the White House. In politics Truman and Hebert were on opposite sides of the fence, but a controversy such as that swarming about the President and his top field commander was another matter. In this context Mr. Hebert said:

I don't believe anybody will seriously disagree with my right
to view with a critical eye anything that Mr. Truman has done.
I was among those who did not support Mr. Truman in the last
election. . . . I have been an articulate and most vocal critic of
President Truman and his administration. . . .

[Hebert then emphasizes that in the presidential election of
1948 a majority of Americans failed to vote.] They failed to
properly protect the most precious property any free man has in
a free nation—the right to vote. How then, can they, a majority of
Americans raise their voices against Mr. Truman's actions [with
regard to MacArthur].

The office of president is the highest in our country. The President is commander in chief of our armed forces, whether his name
is Truman, Taft, or Lincoln. The sanctity of the office is to be
preserved to our people and in the eyes of the world, at the cost
of even disposing of the world's greatest general.

[It must be definitely and clearly understood that] no matter
how great in stature an American general becomes, he is still sub-
ordinate to the President of the United States no matter who that
President is just so long as he holds office under the terms of the
Constitution.[64]

In calm, reflective language the Congressman told his constituents:

Emotional denouncement of the dismissal of General Mac-
Arthur and hysterical demands for the impeachment of President Truman are not the answers to the problem.

The answer lies in the determination of our people . . . never
to again fail to exercise their right of ballot. Proper election of our
public officials is your responsibility and my responsibility and we
cannot escape it.[65]

In a typical response to one of so many letters from his constituents criticizing President Truman's action in dismissing General MacArthur, Congressman Hebert wrote:

I can very well sympathize with your feelings in the matter of
the Truman-MacArthur controversy. It is tragic that we should
lose the services of so great and able a general at this time, but let

me urge that none of us be guilty of emotionalism when sound thinking and sober judgment are so badly needed. More important than the dramatic impact caused by General MacArthur's dismissal, is the necessity for the people to thoroughly understand what has brought about this crisis. I believe this incident should make every American realize that the only way we can have the kind of leadership this country deserves, is for each one of us, individually, to zealously exercise the right of ballot on election day.

Mr. Truman, in dismissing General MacArthur, exercised his Constitutional right, but a majority of our fellow citizens failed to exercise their Constitutional right on last election day, and didn't even take the trouble to go to the polls and vote. Therein lies the real cause for the confusion which exists in our country today, a country where we have inflated currency and deflated morals because of mediocre leadership.[66]

He agreed with many Americans that at the moment the leadership in Washington was not of the highest quality but there was a reason for that.

It is tragic that in this hour of crisis we have such mediocre leadership which borders on complete lack of any degree of leadership.

But we cannot escape the fact that this leadership of mediocrity was designated by the American people either by lack of interest or lack of understanding of their responsibility.[67]

It was due, however, to the decline in the popularity of the Truman program rather than to the Truman-MacArthur controversy that Hebert attributed the passage of the Twenty-second Amendment to the Constitution, limiting to two terms a man's tenure in the White House.

Mr. Hebert noted two reasons for the passage of the Twenty-second Amendment. He said:

I subscribe to the prohibition against any individual being elected president more than twice.

The Twenty-second Amendment is the history of practically all restrictive legislation—the history of the necessity of mandatory legislation to curb abuses.

If Roosevelt [F.D.R.] had not pointed up the dangers of eventual dictatorship through his actions there never would have been placed on the pages of our Constitution such a restrictive measure. . . .

[Hebert also saw the decline in popularity of the Truman program as a reason for passage of the Twenty-second Amendment.]

President Truman may decide not to run for re-election. The new Amendment gives him an 'out,' if he wishes to take it. He can merely say he believes in living up to the spirit of the Constitution as amended.

Such a declaration in itself from President Truman, in the light of his record as president, would be like a fresh breeze in a smoke-filled room.

Maybe it is too much to hope for but hope does spring eternal in the human breast, I am told.[68]

From all the discussion about proper leadership for America as the country moved into the 1950's, Mr. Hebert concluded:

General Eisenhower is the one living American within my sphere who has the complete confidence of the American people at this moment. I, for one, am willing to be guided and influenced by his advice and counsel and recommendations.[69]

Indeed, Mr. Hebert's admiration of General Eisenhower stemmed from the days of World War II and the immediate post-war period. As a result of several contacts with the General and subsequent conversations, Mr. Hebert was of the opinion that he was the leader that America needed. The election of November, 1952, indicated that a majority of American voters shared Mr. Hebert's opinion. Following Eisenhower's election, the Congressman commented that

His genius for inducing men of diverse interests and backgrounds to work together in a common cause is going to be put to its severest test.[70]

At any rate, a new political climate was descending on Washington. Gone would be the man from Missouri who

. . . until the very last minute of his White House occupancy never ceased being the petty partisan precinct politician.[71]

If there was any one explanation for the Republicans replacing the Democrats in the White House, Hebert concluded that it could be summed up in one sentence:

> The voters were sick and tired of the corruption and bungling foreign policy of the Truman Administration.[72]

In the summer of 1952 Dwight Eisenhower defeated Senator Robert A. Taft of Ohio for the Republican party's presidential nomination. Just a year later the man that many people referred to as "Mr. Republican" was dead. Concerning Taft, Hebert said:

> Robert Taft was the rallying point for a great sincere segment of political thought in this country; he stood as a balance wheel for the conservative wing of his party, for those who hated the New Deal concept of Big Government. For this he was often called 'reactionary.' Yet, Senator Taft was a true liberal in the sense that he based his stand on fact, and when confronted with evidence to the contrary, he could change his mind and alter his stand.[73]

The night before President Eisenhower's first inauguration, Mr. Hebert, after noting that Franklin Roosevelt had come to office in 1933 with his "New Deal" and that Harry Truman had followed in 1945 with his "Fair Deal," told the people of New Orleans:

> In the last twenty years many Americans have come to believe that what we really got was a 'raw deal' and tonight offer up the fervent prayer that on tomorrow the American people . . . will begin to get a 'square deal.'[74]

On Partisanship

Over the years of Mr. Hebert's service to the people of the First District of Louisiana, there has occurred on the floor of Congress many a political battle. Some of the major issues of the 1940's, 1950's and 1960's have already been discussed. Regardless of the issue, as has been indicated, Hebert has kept one thought upper-most in his mind and that is service to his constituents and to the American people. Sufficient evidence of his partisan independence has been demonstrated in a foregoing section of Chapter IV. On the other hand, there have been issues during his career that found Mr. Hebert to be quite partisan. Throughout debates on certain issues, Hebert has remained firm because of his long understanding of the problem in relation to his constituency, his state, and his country. In some respects, then, he has demonstrated himself to be a son of his region of America.

Since 1954, for example, most Southerners have been less than enthusiastic about certain decisions of the Supreme Court. Indeed, in the decade and a half that has passed since the school desegregation decision of 1954, life for the ordinary Southerner has undergone remarkable if not radical change. As a result, many people have come to the conclusion, Southerners as well as others, that the Supreme Court has gone beyond the scope of its functions and has entered into the realm of legislating by judicial decree. Few thinking Americans have failed to let the thought enter their minds that often Court appointees have been selected for political reasons. Hebert recognized the intensification of this trend as early as 1954, long before some Senators found sweet political music in a debate involving the qualification of Court nominees. In 1954 Hebert said:

> Ways must be found to check the tendency of the Court to disregard the Constitution and the precedents of able and unbiased judges to decide cases solely on the basis of the personal predelictions of some of its members to political, economic and social questions.
>
> The Court has flagrantly abused its judicial power. It has become a plain tool and political arm of the Executive branch of the government. . . .
>
> The Court's verdict is the most serious blow that has yet been struck against the rights of the states in a matter vitally affecting their authority and welfare.[75]

A month later Hebert attacked the Court's intrusion into matters affecting the Federal relationship. He said:

> The Supreme Court seems, in the last decade, to have made a game of seeing how many domains traditionally reserved for the States it can turn over to the Washington bureaucrats.[76]

Most Southern congressman, along with many Northern and Western representatives, are most acutely conscious of the federal relationship of the government of the United States. Unfortunately for the Union, however, in the last thirty years or so the so-called liberal segment of American politics has been successful in portraying defense of the federal arrangement as something peculiarly Southern. These liberals have interpreted States rights as being, at best, nothing more than a political platitude of the nineteenth century. Hebert appreciates that the distorted interpretation and jargonistic approach of most pseudo-liberals to the American political system is simply a manifestation of the current liberal fad of equating the traditional with evil. Indeed, Mr. Hebert has keenly observed a definite trait among so-called liberals. He expresses it this way:

> You know, it is too bad that so many people who term themselves liberals really have no time at all for a person who supports opposite views.[77]

The fact remains, in spite of the advocates of strong centralized government, that our political system is built upon a federal structure and those persons who so ardently defend that political system really do not care about the cliches of misguided individuals. Hence, let the issue be termed "States rights" and continue with an examination of Hebert's regard for the federal structure.

Mr. Hebert holds that the federal arrangement is fundamental to the continuation of true freedom in America. To this end he has said:

> States Rights and sovereignty . . . are as basic and as elemental to the continued existence of a free government as the Ten Commandments are fundamental to the existence of religion itself.[78]

At no time during his life, and particularly throughout his congressional career, has F. Edward Hebert ever regarded States rights as a sectional matter. At no time has he ever interpreted the federal arrangement as being peculiarly Southern. On the contrary, he has consistently maintained that

> The fight for States Rights is not a Southern or a sectional fight, but a fight involving a principle and an ideal of government which affects the East as much as the South, which affects the West as much as the South and which affects the North as much as the South.[79]

Of those who have made light of the rights of the several states, Hebert has said:

> While pseudo patriots, with bleeding hearts, scream from the housetops about the rights of minorities and lift their anguished voices against so-called discrimination, they advocate in the same breath legislation curbing the individual states (which are certainly the minorities of the whole nation) of their rights and attempt to foist on all the people their own pet schemes and plans even if the people themselves do not want them. . . .
>
> State sovereignty is the real issue involved—the right of the states to function as such, their right to function without dictation from a centralized government.[80]

Hebert could see the growing tendency during the New Deal and Fair Deal years to place more and more authority in the hands of the Washington bureaucrats. In 1953, following Congressional approval of the tidelands oil bill, which was a certain acknowledgement of the rights of the states, Hebert commented:

> In the last twenty years the Federal government has usurped many functions that rightfully belong to the States. Congress made one significant step toward restoring States Rights when it enacted the tidelands oil bill.
>
> But the New Deal-Fair Deal administrations committed many more sins against States Rights in their drive for centralized government. In order to maintain their policies of spend and waste—in their desire to elect and elect—they invaded the State taxation systems.

The New Deal-Fair Deal administrations helped bring governmental poverty to states and municipalities by charging into States . . . and slapping Federal taxes on revenue sources that normally belong to the States.[81]

Only toward the end of the 1960's did it become apparent to the Nixon Administration that the Federal government was depriving the States and municipalities of monies needed for their own operation. In 1969 President Nixon, speaking of a New Federalism, proposed the gradual return of some Federal tax revenues to the States. Hebert had recognized the problem fully sixteen years before. America's cities might have a completely different look today, and there might be fewer slums if the anti-States rights people had stopped shouting long enough in the 1950's to hear the warning of men like Congressman Hebert.

The same foresight was demonstrated by Hebert in still another area that was seen as a liberal Utopia in the 1950's and 1960's but which has become a rallying cry for the discontented of the late 1960's. That is the issue of welfare. In 1954 Hebert could discern that what the average person wants is not welfare but the ability to make a living. Unfortunately for so many welfare recipients, no national administration of the 1950's or 1960's, with the possible exception of the Nixon Administration, was prepared to accept that interpretation. It was far too easy to spend and spend and elect and elect. A year after the first Eisenhower inauguration, Hebert said:

> In the face of history America today flirts with softness. Over the past two decades, the philosophy of government has changed. Instead of government policies that inspire individual initiative, we have to be babied and pampered into the feeling that all we need to do is go on living, and a paternalistic government will take care of everything for us.[82]

One of Hebert's favorite undertakings is the sponsoring of a medical academy. He first mentioned the idea in 1949 when he said:

> My suggestion—which I repeat and which is very much to the

point, is simply this—let the Federal government provide for a Federal Medical School, similar in pattern of operations to West Point and the Naval Academy.[83]

Throughout the years Mr. Hebert was worked untiringly for a national medical school. He has made it clear, however, that his proposal is in no way linked to socialized medicine. In this light, he has said:

We must sell the American public on the idea of the necessity of such an academy which should also merit the support of the doctors and dentists of this country. This is neither socialized nor federalized medicine, to which I am unalterably opposed. It is a plan which will relieve the draft of civilian doctors and dentists, and which will provide more of both. . . .

This is a large problem [the shortage of doctors]. This proposed Armed Services Medical Academy is not the complete answer, but it is a step in the right direction.[84]

Certainly one of the most important pieces of legislation to come before Congress during the 1960's was the Civil Rights Bill of 1964. As the bill was debated on the floor of the House of Representatives, Hebert told his constituents:

This civil rights bill is the most irresponsible piece of legislation ever introduced and considered by the Congress of this nation.[85]

Furthermore,

This civil rights bill is the seed of destruction of the very form of government that those who have gone before us have laid down their lives to preserve. It is a complete surrender of individual rights—it is a complete capitulation to a form of government that wants to control almost our thoughts.[86]

What was objectionable about the bill? For Hebert the bill had a fundamental failing. He told a television audience:

This bill takes away the constitutional rights of 90% of our people—constitutional rights which they have enjoyed since the Constitution was written and adopted.[87]

Indeed, he continued:

This is one of the most far-reaching pieces of legislation that perhaps will ever be passed by Congress in the history of the nation. It will destroy the last vestige of individual rights in this country of so-called majority rule.[88]

Mr. Hebert concluded, however, that the bill would pass both houses of Congress because it was good politics in an election year. But when one cut away the political platitudes associated with the bill's promotion, the stark fact remained there for everyone to see. Mr. Hebert expressed the fact this way:

While the bill supposedly grants rights to minorities, it takes rights from the majority.[89]

Shortly after the passage of the civil rights measure, Mr. Hebert received a letter in which the writer said that he was confused concerning Mr. Hebert's reasons for voting against the proposal. In reply the Congressman said:

I am opposed to all Civil Rights proposals and I voted against the Civil Rights Law because I do not believe it is just. I do not believe it is fair. I do not believe it is equitable. I do not believe it is valid.

Now, if you find any sophistry or semantics in that [statement], make the most of it.[90]

Politics aside, Hebert sees no need for the so-called civil rights legislation, for as he has pointed out time and again:

The Bill of Rights is not a white man's bill of rights, it applies to the Negro too.[91]

Perhaps someday, when it is no longer politically profitable for politicians to tinker with the rights of individuals, someone will remember Hebert's remarks concerning the chartered rights of all Americans.

Hebert has been as outspoken and to the point on many of the other issues that confronted Americans in the 1950's and 1960's. As America inexorably prepared for the Space Age, there were those persons who, "in the winter of our discontent" in the late 1960's could not bring themselves to lift their eyes to the heavens —to the future. They complained that the space program was too costly. Perhaps these people were expressing a genuine concern but there were probably many among them who, had they been living in 1492, would have complained bitterly that Columbus' proposed voyage was a useless and exorbitant waste in view of the slums of Madrid and Barcelona. At any rate, for many individuals no matter how monies are spent—it is always for the wrong purpose. Mr. Hebert has recognized the value, indeed the inevitability, of the space program. With regard to it, he has said:

> I do believe that it is a short-sighted policy for anybody to decry the space program for its costs and attempt to compare it with the Great Society throwaways. . . . If I have to chose between the two, I have no hesitancy in telling you that the most important thing before the country today, outside of the Vietnamese situation . . . is the fact that we must continue the space program and we must open these vistas to new developments in science.[92]

Hebert has always been interested in technological and scientific development. Two examples come to mind of his respect for these developments. Both incidents occurred in 1946. After being in Astoria, Oregon, on official business, Hebert, along with other congressmen, returned to the nation's capital by airplane. He described the flight for his constituents.

> On our return to Washington from Astoria your Congressman made a non-stop transcontinental flight from the Pacific to the Atlantic coast in eleven hours and fifty-five minutes. It was a thrilling experience.[93]

The same year Hebert discussed the navy of the future.

> The plans contemplate strengthening of the present-type navy . . . and developing for the most distant future a combat force of the Buck Rogers type.
> This long-range program envisages revolutionary submarines, atom-propelled . . . and extensive use of guided missiles.

There is every prospect of a radically new type submarine—probably employing atomic energy—which could proceed for weeks at a time completely submerged at higher speeds than our present subs.[94]

The year was 1946—the future was not so distant.

Miscellaneous Issues

Over the years, in his usual forthright manner, Congressman Hebert has voiced a decided opinion on issues that faced the American people at a particular moment. What follows, then, is a montage of statements issued over the years regarding a myriad of issues.

Concerning repeal or amendment of the Taft-Hartley Labor Relations Act, Hebert wrote:

> When I voted for the bill originally, I was motivated entirely by what was in the best interests of the laboring man in the ranks. I believed then, and believe now, that this legislation was in the best interests of the American laboring man, and the American people, and for that reason I voted for it. Since the enactment of the legislation and its subsequent application, I have found no sound reason to change my opinion.
>
> There are certain features of the law, however, which I do not like, and would vote to amend or repeal. . . . I disagree with that part of the Act which makes it mandatory for union officials to sign non-Communist pledges, while not exacting the same demand from management. Here again is exemplified my position, not only on this phase of the Act, but on all labor-management legislation. My position is quite simple and quite clear. I believe that one law should be applicable to both labor and management and that neither labor nor management should have any law applied to one and not to the other under which provisions both are required to live.[95]

With reference to his attitude toward organized labor, Hebert has said:

> I believe in collective bargaining and I believe in organized labor, but I believe in freedom in the ranks of organized labor as much as I believe in freedom in other areas of our civilized life.[96]

Concerning the press, the Congressman has said:

Freedom of the press is freedom to tell the truth. It is also the freedom not to tell the truth.[97]

As a former newspaper reporter I have always been alert and sensitive to reporting the news accurately in order that those who read and depend on the newspapers might have the full knowledge of what is factually the case.[98]

Freedom of the press and freedom of the air can be enjoyed only so long as freedom of that unlimited power is recognized by those in whose hands it reposes.[99]

With regard to some television reporting, Mr. Hebert has said:

The second most important problem [in the United States, following permissiveness] as I see it is the viciousness and insidiousness of the propaganda machines that are brainwashing our American people today. I believe the most vicious instrumentality of destruction and propaganda is the television, and I'm not talking about our local stations.[100]

Concerning electoral reform, Mr. Hebert has offered the opinion that

At first blush I would favor a proposition [for reform of the Electoral College] which would more equitably express the views of the majority in Presidential elections. It is rather incongruous that senators and representatives should be elected by a direct vote of the people, and yet the chief executive, the president, should be elected by remote control, namely, through the mechanism of the Electoral College. It is quite obvious that if we are to have a pure republican form of government, a majority should prevail. Under our present system, such is not the case. In several instances, as you will recall, we have had minority presidents, including Mr. Truman. Very few people realize it, but Mr. Truman did not receive a majority in the Electoral College. It becomes apparent, therefore, that a study of the present system is much needed. Whether or not the Lodge amendment is the answer, I cannot say with finality at this time. It is quite a complicated device, and I do not know if it would solve the problem and achieve the result intended.[101]

Later he said:

There's been a lot of talk, usually just before election time, about our young people. They are extolled as the backbone of our country, our future leaders. . . .

Yet, we've never let the young people themselves have a say in the policies and conditions which they will have to deal with a few years from now.

There is no reason why eighteen-year-olds should not be allowed to vote.[102]

Concerning Israel and the Middle East situation, the Congressman has said:

I have always believed that the Jews have every right to Palestine. I believe that the Jews have every right to establish a homeland of their own and a right to work out their own destiny.[103]

Following the Six Day War in June, 1967, Hebert spoke of the Middle East situation in these terms:

If anything in the Middle East is settled, it is going to be settled not because of the United Nations, but in spite of the United Nations. And no matter what peace or what settlement, or conclusion comes out of the whole situation, the United Nations will have no directional influence, will have no enforcement powers to bring order out of the chaos. It will have to come from the confrontation of the heads of state and the direct negotiations between the belligerents.

The United Nations can do nothing [about the Middle East situation] and has only provided a sounding board for those who want to spew the propaganda of their individual nations. . . . So what do we really have. We have the greatest television show, with a captive audience presented *ad nauseaum*, to the American people. And who pays the bill? You pay the bill.[104]

Hebert's realism is clearly developed in the following selection on the subject of disarmament.

There is nothing inconsistent in my views in voting for this [Disarmament Agency]. I believe in letting these people sit around a table and talk about disarmament. I am not so confused or so naive as to think that we are going to disarm, nor do I advocate disarmament because I know it is not a realistic situation. But, I cannot deny anybody the right to discuss something that we would all like to have, if it was realistic. All this Disarmament Agency can do is talk, and as long as people talk they cannot fight. I certainly do not subscribe to these wild-eyed movements, but I certainly do not want to deny anybody the privilege of discussion.

If I must draw a parallel with the Disarmament Agency, I might say it would be just as illogical for me to deny the right of the individuals to sit aroud a table and discuss the elimination of sin. Now you and I know that sin is going to be with us as long as there will be human beings on earth, and you and I know that men are going to fight as long as there are two people on earth, but certainly neither you nor I, I am sure, would want to deny anybody the right to discuss the possible mitigation of these evils.[105]

On February 9, 1968, Mr. Hebert voiced his opinion of the *Pueblo* incident in a letter to a constituent. He wrote:

My opinion is that we should have struck swiftly and immediately when the *Pueblo* was hijacked to get the ship and its men out of there. When we didn't strike immediately, we lost the advantage that such a move would have had. Now we have no choice but to go through diplomatic channels, but after a reasonable time if such efforts fail, we should use every means at our command to go in there and get the *Pueblo* and its crew. I am damned tired of this country being 'blackmailed' by Communist countries.[106]

Finally, there is that statement made by the Congressman early in his career that has come to be somewhat of a guideline for that career.

The true test of greatness is to be found in the victor and loser who, after the battle, can accept the verdict and join hands in full cooperation for a common cause.[107]

CHAPTER V

LETTERS AND ANSWERS

THROUGHOUT THIS STUDY of the political philosophy of F. Edward Hebert, the author has relied upon excerpts from speeches, addresses, and letters of the Congressman over the past thirty years. Presented below, however, are transcripts of correspondence between Mr. Hebert and concerned citizens relating to political issues of the day. In the course of his reply the Congressman further elucidates his political philosophy. The arrangement of the letters in Chapter V is designed to correspond, generally speaking, with the topics presented in chapters I through IV.

On Patriotism

On May 5, 1967, a representative of the Young Men's Business Club of New Orleans wrote to Congressman Hebert concerning legislation on the subject of flag burning.[1] Mr. Hebert replied:[2]

Dear Fred:

Thank you very much for your letter of May 5 concerning legislation on the subject of flag burning.

There are approximately fifty bills being considered by the House Judiciary Committee. What will come out of it, I do not know. But I will support any law which makes it a Federal crime to desecrate the flag of the United States.

As far as the other law to which I addressed myself is concerned, I find there are sufficient laws already on the statute books—Section 12 of the Selective Service Act and Section 2388 of the U. S. Code 18.

The frustrating thing in this area, however, is that the Department of Justice refuses to prosecute under the law on the basis that the First Amendment is violated, and says also that no effective law can be written. To this I offered the observation that where there is no desire to implement a law there can never be an effective law. The Justice Department stands indicted for dereliction.

With kindest regards,

Sincerely,
F. EDWARD HEBERT

Later in May, 1967, a group of Veterans of Foreign Wars in New Iberia, La. wrote to Mr. Hebert deploring the desecration of the American flag by certain individuals. The veterans appealed to Mr. Hebert to urge Congress to take some action to prevent malicious abuse of the American flag, and move in the direction of restoring peace and tranquility in the land.[3] Mr. Hebert replied: [4]

Dear Mr. Hebert:

May I compliment you for rising up in protest against the burning of the American flag by unpatriotic and disloyal individuals who would have anarchy replace law and order in this country.

I assure you I am in full accord with your thinking and I shall support legislation making it a crime to desecrate the flag.

With kindest regards.

Sincerely yours,
F. EDW. HEBERT

On Americanism and Race

In the spring of 1949, Mr. C. C. Dejoie, Jr., president and managing editor of *The Louisiana Weekly*, suggested in a letter to Congressman Hebert that

If the South is to develop to its fullest capacity, its leaders, white and black, are going to have to know and understand one another with mutual respect instead of indulging in a lot of name calling that accomplishes no good.

Mr. Dejoie further suggested that he might meet Hebert for an exchange of ideas. In the meantime, the editor was forwarding some editorials concerning a recent radio address by the Congressman.[5] The Congressman replied: [6]

Dear Sir:

Of course I am ready at any time to discuss the problems of any group of my constituents, and will be most pleased to discuss the situation of the Negro in New Orleans with you upon my return to Louisiana, provided the discussion is conducted and maintained on a level of understanding, and a desire for cooperation and results.

I cannot reconcile the tenor of your letter, which is commendable, to the manner in which my radio address was handled in your newspaper. The manner in which it was handled was in direct contradiction to what you subscribe to in your letter. If you will look at the head of the story you will find it was an inflammatory head of ridicule which could lead to nothing less than added misunderstanding and prejudice. In fairness, however, I must say the story itself was properly handled, but the head destroyed any thought of fairness and lack of bias.

It is interesting to note, in view of your observations, that every single piece of correspondence I have had with representatives of Negro organizations has originated with officers or spokesmen of the organization involved, and each has been pitched on a tone of ill-temper, bad manners, and discourteous language. It is only natural that each should have been treated in kind by me because where I do not receive respect I do not give it. It is further significant that of the hundreds of letters I receive from Negroes, I have never yet received a discourteous one from an individual, while on the other hand, I have never received a courteous one from an organization.

Yours very truly,
F. EDW. HEBERT

During the integration crisis in Mississippi in 1962, a resident of New Orleans wrote to Congressman Hebert asking him to condemn Governor Ross Barnett of Mississippi for law breaking and rebellion against lawfully constituted authority, namely the Federal courts.[7] Mr. Hebert replied: [8]

Dear Winter:

I am sorry I did not make myself clear in my reply to you of October 3, but I do not believe that Federal troops should be used to enforce a court order such as was done in Mississippi. I am not new in this thinking because a student of history such as yourself will know that Thomas Jefferson and Andrew Jackson both disagreed with Supreme Court decisions and refused to follow them, so I think I am in good company in taking my stand alongside them.

If I had confidence that this was still a government of law and not of men, I perhaps would be more understanding, but unfortunately this country has drifted into a country of men and not of law as reflected in Supreme Court decisions, where laws have been written and not interpreted. Recently President Kennedy made a statement to some foreign students at the White House to the effect that the Constitution of the United States really didn't mean anything more than the interpretation given it by the men who interpret it. This, to me, was one of the most shocking things I have ever heard in my life. Of course, I do not approve of disobeying any law that one does not agree with personally. But unfortunately the Supreme Court is writing the laws instead of interpreting them as passed by the proper body, the Legislative body, which is charged with that responsibility. But, this discussion could go on and on and you and I could not agree on it, but I respect your opinion and I know that you respect mine.

I deplore the fact that such instances as Mississippi and Little Rock occur, but they were generated not by men of good will but by politicians, both Republicans and Democrats, who want to use the Negro as a means of getting block votes in other sections of the country without regard for the traditions, customs and mores of our section of the nation. Nobody is more sympathetic and understanding toward the colored man than I am. I believe he has every right for an education and for an opportunity to earn a living, but I do not believe demagogic politicians have either a moral or legal right to use these people as political bait.

With warmest personal regards.

Sincerely yours,
F. EDW. HEBERT

Shortly after the assassination of Dr. Martin Luther King in April, 1968, Congressman Hebert issued a statement in which he deplored the murder of the civil rights leader, but added that it was his belief that King had preached the use of violent tactics under guise of non-violent crusade. This statement elicited considerable comment, pro and con, from around the country. One such comment emphasized that Mr. Hebert's statement was "a mistake on the part of your thinking. A man of your position with thoughts like those should not be a leader." [9] Mr. Hebert replied: [10]

Dear Miss Smith:

I can well understand your feelings as expressed in your letter of April 8, which obviously are motivated by a wrong conception of what is right and what is wrong.

My appreciation of an elected official is one who speaks the truth and is guided by his own conscience as to what is right and what is wrong, and is not guided by coloring the truth and playing upon the emotions and hysteria of the people.

In referring to my statement you fail to mention that I said I denounce murder and that I would never condone it. Murder does not solve anything.

As far as Martin Luther King is concerned, all you have to do is look at his record and the record of violence which followed in his wake everywhere he went. It would take many pages for me to cite his record here but if you are truly interested in separating fact from fiction you can go to any library or refer to any newspaper's files and you will find out that he aroused people to violence. As a typical example, the very speech the major networks used to saturate the air following his death contained the closing lines, 'Mine eyes have seen the glory of the coming of the Lord.' This sentence is taken from the 'Battle Hymn of the Republic' which was the fighting song of the Northern troops during the Civil War. If this is not arousing to violence, I do not know what is.

The very last speech that he made, which strangely enough has not been reproduced or referred to, denied the law and urged his followers in Memphis to ignore the Federal injunction and take the law into their own hands. If this is not violence I do not know what violence is.

As far as my prejudice is concerned, I have eleven positions on my congressional staff of which three are filled by Negroes. One of my three patronage positions is filled by a Negro and at the present time I have nominated a Negro to the Naval Academy. Also, I was the first Southern Representative to employ a Negro Field Representative.

I have replied to you at length because I recognize and respect your sincerity and I have great respect for the school which you attend [Xavier University]. It is my firm belief that sincere people such as yourself should be informed of the facts and not left to draw their conclusions from hearsay. In view of these facts I am sure you will want to re-evaluate your opinion of me.

With kindest regards.

Sincerely yours,
F. Edw. Hebert

Another comment expressed the thought that the writer "was shocked but not surprised at hearing your remarks on the death of Dr. Martin Luther King. They were the ultimate in tastelessness, and eminently twisted and destructive." The correspondent continued, "I . . . am ashamed for you, for my district, for New Orleans, for Louisiana, and for America." [11] Mr. Hebert replied: [12]

Dear Mr. Keefer:

This will acknowledge your letter of April 7, which incidentally, I had already read in the paper.

While I certainly respect your right to express yourself, I must disagree with you as to the role that Martin Luther King played in creating violence in this country. To begin with, and as usual in such cases, you are referring to just two sentences of what I said. I made the definite statement that I could not condone acts of violence such as murder, and I do not condone them. I think the murder of Martin Luther King was a dastardly and cowardly act. I believe in a country of ballots and not of bullets.

I must call your attention to the so-called 'promised land'

speech which was repeated over and over again by the TV media following the murder of Martin Luther King. I direct your attention to his words, 'Mine eyes have seen the glory of the coming of the Lord,' which you are well aware are from the 'Battle Hymn of the Republic,' and which was the fighting song of the North during the days of the Civil War. This music was repeatedly used to spur on the Union Army and to incite the army into fighting for the cause in which it believed.

I must further direct your attention to the last speech which Martin Luther King made in Memphis in which he defied the Federal Courts and proclaimed to everybody that he did not recognize a legal injunction.

I must further direct your attention to the fact that Martin Luther King was a participant with Stokely Carmichael at the rally held in New York in which the crowd at the meeting was urged to ignore the law and defy the draft, and at which the American flag was burned.

I must also direct your attention to the fact that in the wake of Martin Luther King's urging of civil disobedience, death followed and senseless murders occurred.

I must also direct your attention to what has happened in this country following the murder of Martin Luther King, where we now find a nation bordering on anarchy, demanding the presence of troops to keep law and order.

Of course, these facts will not change your opinion; but I stand by my position of the proper evaluation of the role which Martin Luther King played in stirring up prejudice, hatred, bigotry among the races, and creating violence.

Sincerely yours,
F. Edw. Hebert

One hundred and eighty degrees from the foregoing comments on Mr. Hebert's statement were those such as the following one which said in part: "I certainly appreciate the fact that you made the public statement on the King issue and in doing so told more truth than most others in our Government are willing to admit. We can always count on you to express your opinion even in light of severe criticism. Thank you." [13] Mr. Hebert replied: [14]

Dear Mrs. Canale:

Thank you very much for your letter concerning my recent statement.

You are most kind and generous in your comments in my behalf, and I hope I will continue to merit your confidence.

With kindest regards,

Sincerely yours,
F. Edw. Hebert

Other writers complimented Hebert on his statement and introduced a discussion of some side effects of the King assassination. For example, there was the individual who asked Hebert to do something "to expose the fear and black-mail tactics that were used on April 9, 1968, to force the closing of [schools] and business establishments." [15] Mr. Hebert replied: [16]

Dear Mr. Denny:

Thank you for your letter of April 12, concerning the threats that were made to schools and businesses to close down in honor of Dr. Martin Luther King.

I deeply appreciate your interest in bringing this to my attention. I realize that there were many such incidents in cities throughout the country. Some cities were ravaged by rioters and looters.

You may rest assured that I will keep fighting for a 'get tough' policy for all people who have complete disregard for law and order.

Again, thanks for your concern. I wish more Americans would be as concerned, then perhaps we could put an end to this senseless violence.

With kindest regards.

Sincerely yours,
F. Edw. Hebert

On Draft, Dissent, Demonstrations and Destruction

Over the years since World War II, but particularly during the years of the Vietnam conflict, one has heard numerous suggestions about the need to develop a volunteer army in the United States.

Such a proposal is, at present, impractical as Mr. Hebert indicates in the following letter.[17]

Dear Mr. Drury:

Unfortunately, due to an administrative error, I failed to respond earlier to your letter concerning the possible establishment of an 'all volunteer Army and Reserve.'

Undoubtedly, everyone in our country, particularly young men of draft age, would be pleased if such a simple solution to the military manpower problem was practical and usable. However, numerous studies designed to explore this possibility have been made by the Department of Defense as well as the President's Commission on the Draft and the civilian Advisory Panel headed by General Mark W. Clark. These studies have all concluded with the judgment that an all-volunteer military force simply is impractical and can not be established.

Notwithstanding the foregoing judgment, I agree that increasing incentives for young men to enter the military services on a full-time career basis is certainly desirable and will approach the 'all volunteer force concept.' The Armed Services Committee of the House of Representatives has made a significant contribution in this direction by enacting into law many service benefits not heretofore recommended by the Executive Branch. For example, in 1965, the Committee on Armed Services doubled the pay increase recommended by the Executive Branch and despite the strongest possible opposition from the Executive Branch and the President, this pay increase was enacted into law. The action taken on the 1965 military pay act has been paralleled in many other respects and hopefully Congress will approach, as nearly as possible, the all-volunteer force concept.

On the other hand, during periods of war or hostilities such as we are now experiencing in Vietnam, it is manifestly impossible to maintain an all-volunteer force. Circumstances such as these obviously require the continuance of our draft law.

Sincerely yours,
F. Edw. Hebert

In November, 1965, one of Mr. Hebert's constituents wrote to the Congressman to make known his deep concern regarding "draft-card burners and anti-American demonstrations in our American universities." [18] Mr. Hebert replied: [19]

Dear Mr. Frey:

Thank you very much for your letter of November 9. I was very pleased to have your comments and agree with you that the only way elected officials will know how the people feel is for the people to express themselves.

I share your views completely, and if you are familiar with my record you already know I have deplored this situation in my public statements and public appearances. The disgraceful activities and demonstrations, not only in the Vietnam situation but also in situations where private property is destroyed, is indefensible and I have spoken out against it.

It is most unfortunate that some of our leading elected officials have urged demonstrations for what they advocated, and all of a sudden are amazed when demonstrations occur favoring movements they do not advocate. The outlandish and disgraceful exhibition by a minority group of students is the result of the attitude of these public officials condoning previous demonstrations.

I can only tell you that I have and will continue to do everything that I can to follow the course which you suggest in your letter.

With kindest regards.

Sincerely yours,
F. Edw. Hebert

Demonstrations and flag burning during 1967 caused a sense of outrage among the vast majority of American citizens that was reflected in their correspondence to their representatives.

Referring to the demonstrations, and particularly to a flag burning incident, one correspondent wrote to Mr. Hebert to express outrage at "our so-called leaders [who] have become so calloused, so indifferent, so complacent, or so insensitive, that they permit such a filthy act to be committed with obvious impunity. Where, in the name of God, is our pride? Our patriotism?" [20] Mr. Hebert replied: [21]

Dear Mr. Dodd:

Thank you for your letter of April 24 concerning the demonstrations in New York City and San Francisco, and the burning of the American flag.

I agree that these demonstrations are disgusting, nauseating, and frustrating, bordering on treason and sedition. The only surprise, however, is that some people are shocked that it has happened.

Such demonstrations are inevitable when the Supreme Court allows criminals to run rampant and through its decisions protects the criminal instead of the victim. This did not start today; it started years ago when the first demonstration and invasion of private property was condoned by the courts, the Department of Justice, and the Administration in the White House.

You may rest assured, however, that in my own individual way I shall continue to voice my protest and continue to denounce such practices, but until a majority of the Congress is willing to stand up and be counted, I am very much afraid the frustration will continue.

With kindest regards.

Sincerely yours,
F. Edw. Hebert

The demonstrations and flag burnings of 1967, as well as similar events that preceded that date, served to provoke an explosive demand by many citizens for an anti-riot law and prosecution of those individuals who would incite to riot. To one such demand Mr. Hebert replied: [22]

Dear Mrs. Mendow:

Thank you very much for your letter of January 20 concerning demonstrations and riots.

I certainly agree with you. I have long advocated that Stokely Carmichael and those of his ilk be imprisoned for preaching treasonous and seditious statements. However, it is up to the Department of Justice to prosecute, and it hasn't. In my opinion, the Department of Justice is derelict in its duties for failing to take action in this area.

Regarding legislation, the House passed H.R. 421, the Anti-Riot Bill, last session. It is currently pending before the Senate

Judiciary Committee. Just how effective such legislation will be remains to be seen.

You may rest assured that I will not give up the fight and will continue to do everything in my power to see that these so-called Americans and law violators are put behind bars.

I appreciate your taking the time to let me have your views.

With kindest regards.

Sincerely yours,

F. Edw. Hebert

Some constituents were concerned with riots in America and any number of other problems. Brother Wilbur of the Holy Cross School in New Orleans wrote to Hebert in March, 1968: [23]

Dear Sir:

Please find enclosed an article concerning the recent postponement of the Open Housing Bill. Drew Pearson indicates that a lobby thwarted the House from working on this important piece of legislation. I have four classes involved in civics and social problems and each class wonders if the recent lobby action hasn't killed the chances for this bill to be approved. And if so, what is the House going to do with this national problem? Time seems to be running out, the boys have only nine weeks of school left and then the summer is here. Can we guarantee them a summer free of riots, etc?

Mr. Hebert replied: [24]

Dear Brother Wilbur:

In replying to your letter of March 27 I will start by answering the last question first.

The only people who can guarantee a summer free of riots are the people who incite the riots and the rioters themselves. The recent Kerner Commission report blames everyone for the riots except the rioters and in effect urges more rioting. I believe in our problems being solved in the Halls of Congress instead of on the streets of our cities. All rioting does is to create more prejudice and hatred and brings us closer to the brink of anarchy and disaster.

Now as to the statements made by Drew Pearson. I have known

Drew for forty years and I would say that he would be the last individual I would look to for authoritative information or advice. Only recently, before the exodus of Mr. Robert McNamara as Secretary of Defense, Drew Pearson reported in his column a conversation with me that never took place.

As to the question of the so-called Realtors' Lobby, there is no doubt that there is a Realtors' Lobby as there is a Civil Rights Lobby, Unions' Lobby, Copper Lobby—you name it, and there is a lobby.

As far as blocking consideration of the Civil Rights Bill is concerned, the Administration has taken the position that it wants a vote yes or no on the Senate passed bill before the Congress recesses for Easter. This ploy is to get a vote before the Members of Congress return to their home districts and get the reaction of their constituency. I am sure that you will agree with me that in representative government, particularly in the House of Representatives, the vote of the members should reflect the opinion of the majority of their constituency. I think this is the American way of doing business, but which the Administration desires to block.

The Administration further wants to obtain fast action on this bill before Martin Luther King leads another march on Washington on April 22nd, which it feels would kill the bill because of the antagonism and animosity being aroused by the riots to which you refer.

It undoubtedly would be of interest to you to know that in my twenty-eight years in the Congress I have never received so many protests against any proposed legislation. As of now the count is running better than 3,000 to 5. The protests have caused me to add to my staff in order to reply to each one individually, but we are still behind in answering all the letters.

As to my position on Open Housing, I am devoting my 'Congressional Report' telecast over WWL-TV on Sunday morning at 10:30 to this problem.

It is always good to hear from you and to know your position on any legislation.

With warm regards.

Sincerely yours,
F. Edw. Hebert

Following the rioting in Detroit in 1967, a New Orleanian of prominence wrote to Mr. Hebert to express the idea that "No man, black or white, has the right to take the law into his own hands— to obey what law he wishes and to refuse to obey others. . . . Any officeholder who hesitates to use the powers of law enforcement promptly and intensively for fear of political backfire is encouraging more and more murder, arson, and rioting." [25] Mr. Hebert replied: [26]

Dear John:

Thank you for your letter of August 8.

My position on the rioting has been clear and is clear. It accomplishes little to say I told you so, but the riots that we are experiencing today began when the Federal Administration condoned and permitted the first sit-in demonstrations and the Supreme Court aided and abetted these demonstrations. Now that the seed is bearing fruit some individuals seem to wonder why.

Little less could have been expected when the Administration and the Supreme Court ignored mobs which halted traffic in the streets of our cities, closed down legitimate businesses, stood in the way of military supply trains, and even sat down in the White House and the Department of Defense. What more could be expected than that which we are getting now?

Be that as it may, and regardless of why, the fact is that we must face the reality of what now exists and use every means at our command to restore law and order in this country. By that I mean *whatever force* is necessary.

With kindest regards.

Sincerely yours,
F. Edw. Hebert

The Johnson Administration decided that there should be a thorough investigation of the causes of the rioting that swept America in the middle sixties. As a result, there was named the President's National Advisory Commission on Civil Disorders. When the Commission's report was released, one individual wrote to Mr. Hebert that "The recent report issued by the President's Fact Finding Committee on Civil Disorders and Riots is an abomination:" [27] Mr. Hebert replied: [28]

Dear Mr. McNeel:

Thank you for your letter of March 5, concerning the report of the President's National Advisory Commission on Civil Disorders.

I think my opinion of this report can be summed up in the one statement which I publicly made and which I repeat here: 'propaganda ad nauseam.'

With kindest regards.

Sincerely yours,
F. Edw. Hebert

One constituent wrote to Mr. Hebert to inform the Congressman that the recommendations of the Commission should not be implemented.[29] Mr. Hebert replied: [30]

Dear Mr. Cutrer:

Thanks very much for your note of October 31 in which you express the opinion that the recommendations of the Riot Commission should not be implemented.

I deeply appreciate your taking the time to let me have your views on this, and I must say that we are in general agreement. I said publicly that the contents of the Riot Commission report could be written the day after the members were appointed. The Commission blamed everybody except the people who did the wrongdoings.

Again, thanks for your interest, and it was good to hear from you.

With all good wishes.

Sincerely yours,
F. Edw. Hebert

As violence and near anarchy erupted around the United States in the spring of 1968, the nation was stunned by the assassination of Senator Robert F. Kennedy. Dr. Merrill Hines wrote to Hebert that everyone at the renowned Ochsner Medical Center of New Orleans was "sad and depressed at the great tragedy that has befallen Senator Robert Kennedy. It is unbelievable what has happened. . . ." [31] Mr. Hebert replied: [32]

Dear Merrill:

Thank you for your letter of June 14 concerning the tragic

death of Senator Robert F. Kennedy and the atmosphere of violence which exists in this country today.

The assassination of Senator Kennedy brings into sharp focus the necessity of returning to law and order in this country, which for too long has bordered on the fringes of anarchy. Much of the blame can be attributed to the Department of Justice, which has refused to enforce the laws which are on the books. And the Supreme Court, through its recent decision, has also played a part in the creation of the current atmosphere.

I certainly do appreciate receiving the views of my constituents, and I am happy that you took the time to write me. Please pass by best wishes on to Dr. Ochsner and all my friends at the Clinic.

With best personal regards.

Sincerely yours,
F. EDW. HEBERT

One often-heard proposal to come out of the sixties, probably as a result of the assassinations of President John F. Kennedy, Dr. Martin Luther King and Senator Robert F. Kennedy, was an appeal for gun-control legislation. On this subject Mr. Hebert presented his views in response to letters from his constituents. Those views are best summed up in the following letter.[33]

Dear Mr. Meers:

Thank you for your letter of June 20 concerning proposed gun control legislation.

I think the solution is for a mutual understanding as to what is necessary for the common good. I don't think anybody can deny that some type of legislation is needed. On the other hand, no one can deny that individuals should have the right of guns to defend themselves, for sporting interests, and other legitimate purposes. The problem revolves around the type of legislation and its restrictions, and I feel certain this will be worked out in the very near future.

The real answer to the problem, however, can be summed up in three words—enforce the law. The Department of Justice has continually refused to enforce the laws which are already on the books. The Supreme Court has also contributed to the atmosphere of disrespect for law and order through many of its recent decisions, which have handcuffed law enforcement people and set criminals free to roam the streets.

You may rest assured that I will continue to do all in my power to reverse this trend. Unfortunately, I am but one man and one vote. I deeply appreciate your interest and your letting me have your views.

With kindest regards.

Sincerely yours,
F. Edw. Hebert

Mr. Hebert's criticism of the Department of Justice was compounded when he was denied the list of names of "volunteer observers" for local elections in Louisiana. He denounced the Department publicly in this instance and expressed his feeling on the subject in the following letter.[34]

Dear Mr. Geldert:

Thank you for your letter of November 2 concerning my stand against 'volunteer observers' for the state election.

I have been engaged in an exchange with the Department of Justice relative to this matter. Assistant Attorney General John Doar has refused to release the information and names I have asked for.

He defies the request of a Member of Congress.

In no way do I intend to persecute the 'little guy' for being an observer. I want to insure that he is not being pressured from higher authority to perform these duties, and I want to make sure that laws pertaining to Federal employees are not being broken. I certainly appreciate your interest in this matter and in receiving your views.

With kindest regards.

Sincerely yours,
F. Edw. Hebert

Hebert's feud with the Department of Justice over those persons engaged in anti-war demonstrations and violence is clearly demonstrated in his reply to a request by a constituent to do something about the treasonous activity of some individuals.[35] Mr. Hebert replied: [36]

Dear Mrs. Bickerstaff:

Thank you very much for your letter of October 18 concerning anti-war demonstrators.

I have been speaking out loud and clear against these rabble rousers and agitators from the very beginning. Unfortunately, the Department of Justice does not agree with me that these persons are preaching treasonous and seditious statements and should be prosecuted. In my opinion, the Department of Justice is derelict in its duties.

Before a House Armed Services Committee hearing, the Assistant Attorney General of the United States told me he was unfamiliar with the statutes under which such people could be prosecuted. Subsequently, I was accused by the press of wanting to do away with the First Amendment of the Constitution and free speech.

You may rest assured of my continued efforts to put these disloyal Americans behind bars where they belong.

With kindest regards.

Sincerely yours,
F. Edw. Hebert

In response to a letter from a New Orleanian regarding the **Department of Justice, Mr. Hebert wrote:** [37]

Dear Mr. Byers:

Thank you for your lettter of May 7 and for the clipping from the Wall Street Journal entitled 'Party on the Spot.'

My opinion of the Department of Justice is that it is the most dangerous department in the Executive Branch of the government. It has condoned riots, lawlessness, demonstrations, and contempt for law and order in this country.

Under Ramsey Clark and his predecessors there has been no intent whatsoever or efforts to enforce the laws on the books. It has continuously flouted the intent of the Congress, made excuses for defiance of the law, and has aided and abetted those who would protect the criminal.

I am sure you have no doubt about how I feel.

I deeply appreciate your interest and your calling this to my attention.

With kindest regards.

Sincerely yours,
F. EDW. HEBERT

Concerning Attorney General Ramsey Clark, one constituent wrote: "It would seem to me that there is more than sufficient evidence available that the present Attorney General, Ramsey Clark, is not carrying out his constitutional duty to enforce the laws of this nation, and I cite for a specific example his continued refusal to prosecute Stokley Carmichael. I would urge you to lead a group of representatives to insist on the immediate resignation of Ramsey Clark by bringing sufficient pressure on the President to either summarily dismiss Clark or force his resignation." [38] Mr. Hebert replied: [39]

Dear Mr. King:

Thank you for your letter of June 14 concerning the lack of law enforcement by the Department of Justice under Attorney General Ramsey Clark.

I have already asked for the resignation of Attorney General Clark, and for some time have openly criticized the Department of Justice for not enforcing the law. In this vein, last year when I questioned Assistant Attorney General Fred Vinson on the subject of not enforcing laws which are on the books, the press accused me of wanting to do away with the First Amendment of the Constitution.

You may rest assured that I will continue to fight and express my opinions about the Department of Justice. Unfortunately, I am but one man and have only one vote, and I seem to be in the minority regarding this matter.

I deeply appreciate your kind words and your taking the time to let me have your views.

With kindest regards.

Sincerely yours,
F. EDW. HEBERT

On War, Peace, Isolation and Collective Security

A basic position adopted by Mr. Hebert on the subject of foreign relations is aptly stated in the following letter.[40]

Dear Mr. Boutte:

I assure you I agree with your estimation of our policy makers, and appreciate having your letter of December 5.

I can best sum up my international position in a phrase which I often use publicly. It is this: 'I first ask myself the question, what is best for America and then I act.' In other words, I am not interested in saving the world at all, I am only interested in saving America, and if it is to the advantage of this country to make certain commitments, then I am in favor of them, and if these commitments are not to the advantage of this country, then I am not in favor of them. I feel very keenly about preserving the strength and integrity of this country first before any attempt is made to save anybody else.

Thank you for writing me and I hope that all good Americans will take as much interest in this country as you have obviously taken.

With kindest regards, I am

Sincerely yours,
F. Edw. Hebert

Perhaps Mr. Hebert's foregoing statement "if these commitments are not to the advantage of this country, then I am not in favor of them," resulted from the astonishment he experienced upon learning that President Roosevelt had entered into secret agreements with the Russians at Yalta concerning the future of the Kurile Islands. Upon learning of the secret agreement, Hebert wrote to Secretary of State James F. Byrnes. He wrote: [41]

Dear Mr. Secretary:

The revelation of the secret pact at Yalta in connection with the Kurile Islands has come as a shock to me as I am sure it has to thousands of other Americans.

I recall most vividly the day the late President Roosevelt appeared before Congress to make his report on Yalta and I can still hear him say, 'There were no secret agreements.'

It appeared to me that he even went out of his way to impress upon the American people that there had been no secret agreements reached at Yalta. Naturally, the revelation of the Kurile commitment causes me to wonder just what other secret deals have been made and how far the American people have been committed to other nations without their knowledge or the knowledge of their elected representatives in Congress.

May I respectfully ask an answer to this simple question?

Are there any other secret deals that we don't know anything about, similar to the Kurile commitment?

If there are I think the proper time to let us know is now. It is time to clear the air. By letting these agreements trickle out one by one all that is done is to fan the fires of suspicion.

Respectfully yours,
F. Edw. Hebert

The Secretary of State replied: [42]

Dear Congressman:

I have your letter of February 4 asking whether there are any 'other secret deals' that we don't know anything about similar to the Kuriles commitment.

I know of no agreement similar to the Kuriles commitment which has not been made public.

For your information, I learned of the agreement as to the Kurile Islands about September 2. The agreement was not on file in the State Department. Upon inquiry, I was advised that there was such an agreement. My understanding was that it was in the form of a record of a conference between Mr. Churchill, Marshal Stalin and President Roosevelt, and that it contained the understanding as to the Kuriles and also the provisions which were thereafter incorporated in the treaty between the Soviet Union and the Government of China.

On September 4 at a press conference, I stated there was such an agreement at Yalta. I had no occasion to make further inquiry into the matter until my return from London last week when I was advised that Under Secretary Acheson had been asked as to whether or not there was a formal agreement signed by the representatives of the three Governments and had answered that he did not have information on the subject.

I immediately inquired and learned there was a signed agreement at the White House.

I was at Yalta but I can understand why I was not aware of the agreement. There were private talks between President Roosevelt, Mr. Churchill and Marshal Stalin, in which private conferences the agreement was reached. However, it was not put in writing until the last day of the Conference, February 11. I had left the previous afternoon in order to return on Admiral King's plane instead of waiting to return by ship.

I can understand President Roosevelt's view. The agreements were, of course, based upon Russia's entering the war. Our military leaders advised me at that time that the Soviet position was that they could not enter the war until ninety days after the surrender of Germany. It would take that time for them to move their armies to the Japanese front.

Our armies were attacking on the Western Front. They needed all the assistance that could come from a simultaneous attack by Russian armies. If the Japanese had learned of this agreement, they would have immediately attacked Russia. That would have necessitated the removal of Russian troops to Japan just when they were starting on the final drive which brought about the collapse of the German army on that front.

We are apt to forget that President Roosevelt died shortly afterwards, April 12, before the end of hostilities in Germany. I assume that after Russia entered the war, or after the Japanese surrender, President Roosevelt would have made public the fact that such an agreement existed.

In any event, I learned of it shortly after the surrender and I made it public within two days after I learned of it.

At the time I accompanied President Roosevelt to Yalta, I was Director of Mobilization, not Secretary of State. In view of the reasons for secrecy I have above suggested, I have no complaint about his not having advised me of the agreement.

I write you at length because of your interest. I repeat that I have no information of any other similar agreement.

Sincerely yours,
JAMES F. BYRNES

Closely associated with the foreign relations of the United

States is the foreign aid program inaugurated after World War II. In those immediate post-war years, Hebert was quite favorable to the program. In time, however, as this instrument of good became an institution of self-perpetuation and deprived this nation of funds, over the years, that could have been wisely put to use on domestic improvement, Hebert became highly critical of most aspects of the program. His views are amply stated in the following letter.[43]

Dear Miss Mier:

Thank you for your letter concerning our foreign aid program.

The Congress managed to cut our foreign aid appropriations by some $200 million last year, and it is hoped that enough votes can be obtained to trim it some more this year.

We have spent millions of dollars in an effort to buy friendship, and I think we have failed miserably. The nations we have given so much to have ignored us and our need for assistance in the Vietnam war. Other countries take our funds and use them against us.

Our entire foreign assistance program needs to be re-evaluated, and we should determine who our true friends are. We cannot continue to support the whole world; we must now consider our plight here at home.

I deeply appreciate your interest and your letting me have your views on this subject. It is heartening to see our youth concerning themselves with the affairs of their government.

With kindest regards.

Sincerely yours,
F. Edw. Hebert

Although Mr. Hebert is decidedly critical of some aspects of the foreign aid program, he is firmly in favor of assisting a nation to the best of our ability once we have committed ourselves to do so. This does not mean to imply, however, that he reserves criticism of such an undertaking. The case in point is Vietnam.

Following the passage of the Tonkin Gulf Resolution by Congress in 1965, Mr. Hebert's office was flooded with mail from people supporting or denouncing American military implication in the Vietnam struggle. Mr. Hebert explains his position in the following letter.[44]

Dear Mr. Pons:

Thank you for your letter of August 11.

Nothing bears heavier on a member of Congress than his decisions on war. I certainly agree with you that moral judgments are inherent in the Vietnam war, but I unhesitatingly disagree with your contention that the actions of the United States are wrong or immoral.

Since you refer to the 'lessons of 20 years ago,' I gladly use this as a point of reference. Twenty years ago the 'moral' nations of the world rationalized away the seizure by the Third Reich of Austria and Czechoslovakia. Both were sovereign nations whose independence had been guaranteed. Hitler proclaimed that these two states were to be part of the Third Reich because of national ties to Germany—whether or not Austria or Czechoslovakia agreed. This is equivalent to North Vietnam's designs for the Republic of South Vietnam.

Appeasement at Munich only whetted the desires of the Third Reich, and Hitler thereupon laid claim to all of Europe.

In Asia, we have the same situation. Communist China has made no efforts to conceal its aim of dominating the continent. It has openly invaded India, and it has openly conquered the independent state of Tibet. Now, through its puppet state of North Vietnam, Communist China intends to crush South Vietnam. If South Vietnam perishes, all other sovereign nations of Asia are ripe for plucking.

To say that the United States is interfering in a 'civil war' is to ignore where the arms shipments come from and from whence the direction of subversion originates. The communist technique of conquering by the euphemistic 'wars of liberation' is all too apparent.

North Vietnamese troops or subversive agents have no more of a *natural* right (as you stated) to be in the independent state of South Vietnam than do Argentines have the right to invade Chile.

Despite the repeated offers of our President to negotiate, North Vietnam has not made one move to withdraw from interfering with the nation of South Vietnam. The United States has long ago, under President Eisenhower, pledged its support to maintaining the independence of South Vietnam. And the United States is keeping that pledge. To do otherwise would be to make a mockery of our similar pledges to the Philippines, and the other sovereign and free nations of Asia.

I fully support our President and the foreign policy he has enunciated in Southeast Asia. I submit that the most immoral act this nation could make would be to allow tyrants, in whatever guise or by whatever means, to overthrow sovereign nations.

I might add, in closing, that Hitler glibly assured the world that Austria and Czechoslovakia were glad to be annexed to the Third Reich. Peking and Hanoi would have us to believe the same of South Vietnam.

With kindest regards.

Sincerely yours,
F. Edw. Hebert

While Congressman Hebert firmly supported President Johnson's decision to commit American men and treasure to the battle for South Vietnam, he nevertheless began an early criticism of the conduct of the war. This growing criticism, based upon the belief that the United States was trying to fight this war "Korean style" —that is, with one arm tied behind the back—becomes apparent in the following correspondence.[45]

Dear Mr. Tharp:

Thank you for your letter of October 13.

I believe my views on the Vietnam situation are well known as they have been expressed both publicly and privately on many occasions. I have always advocated spending as much money and putting as many men into the war as it takes to win and win quickly.

We cannot pull out of Vietnam now. The war we are engaged in is necessary for the salvation and protection of America as we know it. A decisive victory in Vietnam is a must. I assure you that I will continue to do everything in my power to achieve victory in Vietnam and end the war as soon as possible so our boys can return home.

Relating to your desire that we accept the Nationalist Chinese troops in helping us in Vietnam, I, too, am in favor of our acceptance, as well as the aid of any others who want to fight on our side.

In connection with your request that I propose a bill calling for the complete termination of all foreign aid to any and all nations that are or have had dealings with Communist countries, this is a matter which is considered by the Congress each year when the Foreign Aid Authorization Bill comes before us. I have continuously opposed our giving aid to such nations, but unfortunately there are not enough members in the Congress who believe as you and I apparently believe.

With kindest regards.

Sincerely yours,
F. Edw. Hebert

As the war continued, Americans tended to divide in opinion on the best approach of our government to the Vietnam situation. Mr. Hebert reveals his views in the following letter.[46]

Dear Mr. Westbrook:

Thank you very much for your letter of March 10.

I can't agree with you more in your description of the manner in which the Vietnamese war is being conducted at the moment. When they list the Hawks and the Doves, I am the loudest of the Hawks.

I have discussed exactly what you have described in your letter time and time again with Secretary McNamara and I cannot subscribe to his viewpoint and I have so told him.

I assure you that I shall continue my efforts along these lines.

With kindest regards.

Sincerely yours,
F. Edw. Hebert

Hebert's devotion to the cause of freedom was in no way diminished as the second year of America's participation in the war came to an end. He wrote: [47]

Dear Miss Daugherty:

Thank you very much for your letter of April 24 concerning the war in Vietnam.

I have always supported our efforts in Vietnam. One may not agree with why we are there or with how the war is being fought, but the fact remains that we are there, and we must fight and we must win.

This war is being fought not for the Vietnamese, not for other peoples, but primarily for ourselves as Americans to safeguard and to protect the way of life into which we are born. And where American boys are giving their all, I will do everything in my power to support them.

I do appreciate your interest in this matter and your taking the time to let me have your views.

With kindest regards.

Sincerely yours,
F. EDW. HEBERT

As the limited (for the United States and her allies) and seemingly endless war in Vietnam dragged on into 1968, Mr. Hebert wrote: [48]

Dear Mr. and Mrs. Haddock:

Thank you for letting me have your views concerning the so-called Civil Rights Bill.

I am unalterably opposed to this vicious piece of legislation and you may be assured that I shall continue to do everything I possibly can to have it defeated.

I can well understand your concern about our involvement in Vietnam. The war in Vietnam is understood by fewer Americans than any war in our history. How we got there is no longer important. The fact is we are there and we must win if we are to stand before the world as the defender of liberty, justice, and freedom.

If we pull out now, those 20,000 Americans who died there will have died for nothing. We must adopt a 'win policy' now and use every means necessary to accomplish the objective. Hanoi cannot be trusted and will not talk peace as the many peace feelers which we have sent forth have been ignored. The only way to get Hanoi to talk peace is to bring the Ho Chi Minh regime to its knees militarily.

Despite this, however, I now feel that if we don't attempt an immediate victory, which I know we can accomplish, then we should get out.

Again many thanks for letting me have your views. It is encouraging to see so many citizens concerned about the policies of their government.

With kindest regards.

Sincerely yours,
F. Edw. Hebert

On Congress

From the beginning of his congressional career, Hebert has insisted that his critics or would-be critics obtain all the facts of a situation before attacking his position. Six months after taking his seat in the House of Representatives, he answered a critic in the following terms.[49]

Dear Mr. Storek:

I would suggest that in the future before you write such letters as you directed to me that you obtain the facts.

At no time during my broadcast on Sunday night over the American Forum of the Air, did I use the name 'Huns' or refer to 'Huns.' Undoubtedly your hearing is very bad or you deliberately wanted to misinterpret my remarks over the radio which were directly to the point of the discussion.

For your information, my name is French and I represent the City of New Orleans in the national halls of Congress and I will continue to represent them for many years to come.

The next time you write a letter, be sure you know what you are talking about.

Yours very truly,
F. Edw. Hebert

Some time later, the wholly unfounded charges which an individual made in a letter to Hebert prompted the Congressman to write: [50]

Dear Mr. Connell:

I was very much interested in your letter of March 2, because it is a typical example of how so many people arrive at wrong conclusions when they are not in possession of all the facts. Obviously, you know nothing about me and my record in Congress because I am sure if you did you would not have written such a letter. Of course, I can well understand that you might not know anything about me or my activities, since you do not live in my district. Whether or not I represent the majority opinion in my district is reflected, I believe, in the fact that I have been re-elected five successive times by overwhelming majorities.

With regard to how much landlords spend or do not spend on their property, that is something which could be debated ad infinitum. If you will take the time to examine the situation you will find, in many instances, landlords cannot spend money because of the high price of labor and materials. I know of my own knowledge of one landlord who had the exterior of one house painted, and the cost wiped out the rent for the entire year. I know of my own knowledge of landlords who get rent in the neighborhood of $25.00 per month, and spend on an average of $50.00 per year having the plumbing fixed, which the tenants themselves break.

Now, apparently you did not even read my statement because if you had you would not have made the remarks made in your letter to me. Nowhere in the statement did I advocate the immediate removal of rent controls. On the contrary, I made the definite statement, and I quote: 'As to complete removal, it is obivous that all controls can't be taken off immediately.'

That is my position, not only on rent controls, but on any government control, and I have no apologies to make for it. I have opposed bureaucratic government, and will continue to oppose it. I have opposed socialized government, and will continue to oppose it. I have opposed having different laws for different people, and will continue to oppose such type of legislation.

In your letter you make this definite and positive statement: 'Your statement that conditions in this area do not warrant further rent control is entirely false.'

At no time have I ever made such a statement, nor is it contained in the news article to which you refer, which I have before me. This is purely a figment of your own imagination, in an attempt to read something which I did not say into something which I did say.

Now, here is something else you obviously don't know about me. I helped write the first rent control law in this country, and

that law today is the one rent control law that is not being attacked. I refer to the rent control law which governs the District
of Columbia, which is administered on a local level, and which is
a good and equitable law. Of course, you would not know about
that, or you would not have gone off half-cocked and written
such a criticism of my position. The District of Columbia is not
under Federal rent control, and that is why the rent law here is
such a success.

Of course I believe you have made the statements which you
have made only because you are not acquainted with the facts,
and that is the reason I am taking this rather lengthy manner of
replying to you.

Sincerely,
F. Edw. Hebert

One correspondent informed Hebert that for years he was under the impression that "Mr. Hebert was no damn good." He continued, "Although my opinion of you has changed radically since
that time, I note with not a little interest that others—supposedly
responsible members of the fourth estate—are making the same
mistake I made; that of judging a man without knowing, or caring
to know, his qualifications.[51] Mr. Hebert replied: [52]

Dear Mr. Schiappa:

It was most kind and thoughtful of you to send such a generous
letter and I want you to know that I deeply appreciate it.

I always appreciate those who see the light in the window and
come into the house where I always have food and drink for them.

With kindest regards.

Sincerely yours,
F. Edw. Hebert

Hebert has, on occasion, received letters similar to the following
excerpt which speaks for itself.[53]

Dear Mr. Hebert:

Because of your past record in Congress, because of your ful-
filled endeavor to see the youths of America murdered on a large
scale, because of your constant and most hearty opposition to the
advances and betterment of labor, and because, at times, you have

shown complete disregard for the American way of life, I wish to make known my absolute decision to vote against you in the approaching congressional election. I will also attempt to support your opposition both materially and financially even though your defeat for re-election for Congress is a foregone conclusion. . . . In the coming election I also wish to reveal some of the letters which you wrote to your constituents branding them as fascists and communists. I believe such letters will suffice to prove to your constituency how you acted as a congressman. They are your letters, contain your signature, and cannot be denied by you in any campaign speeches.

Mr. Hebert replied: [54]

Dear Mr. Klein:

I assure you your letter was most gratifying. I deeply appreciate your very frank and open expressions. As I have noted before, you and I have nothing in common, not even intellect.

I assure you I desire to assist you in your campaign as much as possible because I know you are a very effective worker, judging by results in the past. If after examining your files you should find missing any of the letters I have written you please let me know and I assure you and I shall be only too glad to supply you with copies. I sincerely hope you do not change your mind about opposing me and offering all letters I have written you to the opposition, as it would be most unfair to the electorate not to let them know what type of individual opposes me.

Sincerely yours,
F. Edw. Hebert

While on the subject of election to office, it might be well to point out here that Mr. Hebert has always strongly supported the two-year term of office for representatives. His views are set forth in the following letter.[55]

Dear Mr. Schreiber:

This will acknowledge your letter of December 14, regarding the introduction of legislation to extend the term of members of Congress to four years from the two years as specified in the Constitution.

This proposal has been advanced consistently for many years in the Congress, and very frankly I do not see any possibility for this change as it would necessitate a constitutional amendment which needs ratification by three-fourths of the States.

Personally, I am opposed to such legislation. The two year term is the last vestige of power which the electorate has over the executive department. This power is vanishing rapidly, and I am opposed to anything which would dilute it even more.

If Congress were elected for either four or six years it would mean the electorate would have to wait four years to express its pleasure or displeasure over the control of the national administration. Taking the results of the last election, without regard to merits or demerits, favor or disfavor, of the results, it would mean if the electorate is not satisfied with the manner in which the president administers his program, it would have to wait four instead of two years to express its disapproval.

As a member of Congress for the past twenty-four years, I have always welcomed the opportunity to go before my constituents each two years to give an account of my service and to learn from them directly whether or not I have functioned in the manner in which they believe I should.

It is interesting to note that the only manner in which an individual can become a member of the House of Representatives is through a direct vote of the people. There is no provision for a line of succession and no provision for appointment to vacancies. Thus the only entrance to the House of Representatives is through a direct vote of the people—which is as it should be.

Of course, I recognize there are many who do not share this view and selfishly there are many who would like to be elected for life and never have to face their constituency. But I do not believe this to be in the best interest of the country.

Thank you very much for letting me have your views, and it was nice hearing from you again.

With kindest regards.

Sincerely yours,
F. Edw. Hebert

The Congressman's views remained unaltered when, some time later, he wrote: [56]

Dear Miss Herbert:

Thank you for your letter of March 6 concerning the two-year term of United States Representatives.

I am strongly in favor of maintaining the two-year term. The House of Representatives is the last link remaining between the people and their government. A representative has to give conscientious thought to his every move, knowing that the people will not forget his actions over a period of two years.

And every two years he has to account for what he has done. Granted, a campaign every two years is a physical and financial strain upon an individual, but these drawbacks are overridden by the merits of the two-year term.

A representative has to keep his finger on the pulse of his district, and because he has to run every two years, he spends time among his constituents. They like the personal contact because they are able to express their views, and they know their representative is listening.

I deeply appreciate your interest in this matter, and I hope the foregoing information is helpful to you.

With kindest regards.

Sincerely yours,

F. EDW. HEBERT

Mr. Hebert's appreciation of his office includes a positive belief in the proposition that a representative must be free to act for his constituency and to do what he believes to be the will of the majority of that constituency. His nonpartisan attitude has already been demonstrated. The following letter, however, lends insight to this issue and describes the difference between an effective and ineffective representative.[57]

Dear Dave:

This is the first chance I have gotten to answer your very kind letter. I wanted to write myself instead of dictating the letter and that is the reason I have been compelled to wait until now.

First of all, I do want you to realize how grateful and appreciative I am of your observations and comments because they were generated by a personal friendship for me. Because of that friendship and your ability to understand me I am sure you can well guess my reaction to many matters.

Whether I am, in the opinion of others, possessed of honesty and integrity does not make much difference. In my own mind and in my own way I attempt to live by those standards. Ever since I have been in public office I have attempted to be honest, fair and forthright in my public statements and conduct. As I suggested to you recently during one of our conversations, the premium placed on hypocrisy, insincerity and downright lying in public office is repugnant to me. It is a price which I do not desire to pay for a seat in the Congress. Now this is not a righteous outburst, it really is not. It is how I feel deeply and keenly.

I am well aware that some people, perhaps many, are critical of me for the attitude which I take in many instances. For the better part, however, I think you will agree with me, that these people are looking for excuses and not reasons to oppose me. Take your friend Clayton Fritchey and the *Item* as an example. They are determined that I shall not return to Congress and there is not a thing they would not do to prevent me from returning, fair or foul. No matter what position I might take or what I might say would be accepted by them. Now mind you, I don't dispute their right to oppose me. Believing in the philosophy of government which they believe, they could not help but oppose me. What I do object to is the flimsy excuses and distorted versions of what I stand for and what I do and say.

Now to be specific. It would be downright dishonest for me to say that I believe New Orleans has a chance to get the new Air Academy. It would be deceitful for me to leave the impression that by saying I would do all I could would mean that there was hope for the selection of New Orleans. I believe it basic to be honest with the people as well as with individuals.

Oh, I know and readily realize and acknowledge that most people don't want to hear the truth and would prefer to be deceived. I don't subscribe to that procedure, however. Then by being honest on a specific case can I be justly criticized for speaking the truth although it is not what is desired to be heard? Look at my actions during my ten years in Congress. I think my efforts have been constructive and my accomplishments speak for what

I believe. How then, by one expression, telling the truth, it can be said that I don't want to get anything for New Orleans?

Take the Port of Embarkation fight as another example. The easy impressive way for the public would have been to make appointments for Chep when he requested them. Have him come to Washington, walk in, shake hands with the big shots, express great interest in retaining the port, issue a statement saying that the proper officials have been contacted. As far as the public is concerned they would have been satisfied but what actually would have been accomplished? Nothing. On the contrary, the arrangements which I made were fruitful and beneficial, I believe. Our strength in this particular case is that unless we can economically justify the port we do not want to gain anything at the expense of economy. Under the idea of not telling the truth and promising everything the procedure would be to insist on a part of the business continuing in New Orleans even if it was economically unsound.

I certainly would not consider you the friend I do if I asked you an opinion and you told me the politic thing instead of the truth. In this particular instance you certainly would not have been a friend of mine if you had written me and said you agreed with my position because it would perhaps be the thing I would want to hear. You were absolutely honest and straightforward in telling me where you think I am wrong and I appreciate your observation because it is an honest observation.

As for as fighting the Truman Administration. The Truman Administration has fought me at every turn. Didn't the Long Administration fight Chep at every turn and didn't Chep fight back at every turn? Certainly Chep could not be accused of hampering the progress of the city because he fought and disagreed with the Long Administration. The fact that he was willing to stand up and fight for what he thought was right won success and admiration for him. He was not condemned but acclaimed and admired. Isn't that the same position in which I find myself? Should I agree with the Truman Administration and refuse to criticize it when I think it is wrong because I put political expediency above honesty of purpose? I don't think so.

Practically, I also recognize the fact that reprisals against the city of New Orleans, if there are to be any, not only affect me but also affect Hale who is wholeheartedly aligned with the Truman Administration and we BOTH represent New Orleans. In other words, from a practical and coldblooded viewpoint, what is worth more to the Truman Administration—almost blind loyalty or loyal opposition. Surely anybody who says X project can't be obtained for New Orleans because of my independence can't also say that X project should not be obtained because of Hale's great influence with the Administration.

After reading this long epistle you more than ever realize how difficult it is to change my way of going, don't you? I still have no terminal facilities. I am sure you understand I just wanted to explain my position to the fullest.

I think the best qualification a candidate can have is the confidence of the people. I would rather people say of me that they can believe me instead of saying I was a cagy politician which I would not consider to be very complimentary.

You know Dave, how I feel and how I react to things. If I acted any differently, I just would not be me.

Again, please know how I appreciated your honest reaction and comment and don't hesitate to tell me anytime what you think about me. . . .

Best ever,
EDDIE

On President Truman

The friction between the Congressman and Mr. Truman's policies was ever present because there was no broad common ground of basic political philosophy upon which the two men could meet. This is undoubtedly best seen in the exchange of letters between Congressman Herbert and President Truman which probably mark the highwater point of their feud. The exchange took place in late 1950 and began when Mr. Hebert wrote the following letter.[58]

Dear Mr. President:

The present crisis [the Korean conflict] in which we are living is naturally of great concern to every American and it is in that connection that I respectfully submit a suggestion to which I hope you will agree.

In these times of indecision and unrest it is most imperative that our people become united and solidified in the common cause of the preservation of our accepted way of life. To that end I suggest that you, as President of the United States, call upon the churches of America, Catholic, Protestant and Jewish, to set aside a Sunday between now and Christmas, to appeal to Almighty God for guidance and wisdom in what I believe to be the Gethsemene of our existence.

I believe that now is the time for our people to set aside whatever differences of opinion that might exist in a unified effort for ultimate success in our fight to continue the freedom of the free peoples of the world. I believe and suggest that the spiritual leaders of our nations be called upon to set aside a Sunday on which the respective pastors shall urge the people of this country to join in prayer to the God of their belief to give to our responsible officials, political and military, the wisdom and the courage, to arrive at the right and proper decisions. At the same time I believe that our religious leaders should explain to their flock the ideals and principles for which we are fighting and for which many are offering the supreme sacrifice.

Certainly we are engaged in a crusade as important as any in which our forebearers ever participated. Our modern crusaders, under the banner of the United Nations, are fighting just as hard and as vigorously and as courageously, to gain the Holy Grail of individual liberty and freedom as any knight who went forth in the armor of his time.

I do hope, Mr. President, that you will see fit to concur in this suggestion, and ask the churches of America to set aside a Sunday prior to Christmas, the feast day of the nativity of the Prince of Peace, to call upon God in this fight against a Godless ideology. And where should the peoples of the world look for help and assistance in a fight against God except to God Himself?

It is my sincere belief that the psychological effect on the American people and the peoples of the world would be a terrific impact in the cause which we all espouse and in a united nation to fight the forces of evil which threaten us at the moment. I hope that I have your concurrence.

Cordially yours,
F. Edw. Hebert

The President replied: [59]

My dear Congressman Hebert:

I appreciated very much your letter of the fifth, and I am enclosing you a copy of my Thanksgiving Proclamation, inviting your attention to the wind-up of that Proclamation beginning, 'NOW, THEREFORE.' I think that effectively answers your suggestion.

I am extremely sorry that the sentiments expressed in your letter were not thought of before November seventh, when the campaign in your State, Utah, North Carolina, Illinois and Indiana was carried on in a manner that was as low as I've ever seen and I've been in this game since 1906.

Sincerely yours,
Harry S. Truman

When the exchange of letters was made public, Congressman Hebert's office was flooded with letters from persons supporting his suggestion for the day of prayer. Excerpts from these letters are presented below.

Dear Sir:

As a good western democrat [*sic*], I have been quite an admirer of your stand on public questions for some time. I hope that this last example of the President's personal stupidity won't make you any more disgusted than it has made the majority of Democrats everywhere.[60]

Dear Sir:

May I offer my congratulations on the wonderful letter you wrote Harry S. Truman. I am not a religious man, but I am sure your thought, if carried thru [*sic*] will go far to unite the American people. . . .

I wouldn't feel too badly, if I were you, but instead, I would consider the source. There is nothing he can do that would surprise me.[61]

Dear Congressman:

May I compliment you on the constructive thought you expressed in your recent correspondence with President Truman and also, on the exemplary way in which you handled yourself in your answer to him.

Your request to him for a day of prayer is certainly timely. . . .

It is unfortunate that the President allowed his political temper to get the better of him. His countrymen will think less of him for it. . . .[62]

Dear Sir:

I just heard of the fine letter you wrote to Pres. [*sic*] Truman asking him to call for a day of prayer in all churches on some Sunday, and the President's shameful answer. He is surely not a statesman but a cheap politician and 1952 can't come too quick to vote him and his gang out.[63]

Dear Sir:

In regard to your request for national prayer—it is unfortunate that Mr. Truman took the attitude he did. As contemptible as it was to me, we must realize that these perilous times may make a confused mind go off on a tangent.

Your idea is the right one. . . .[64]

Dear Congressman:

Your suggestion that the President of the United States set aside a Sunday between December 5th and Christmas on which Sunday the people of the United States would appeal to Almighty God for guidance and wisdom to assist them to obtain peace in this world—is a splendid one. . . .

'Tis sad but true that we have several men in office who were elected as leaders of the people, but regardless of the serious condition of the world, they cannot forget for one second the political party angle.[65]

Dear Congressman:

I feel that the nation is indebted to you for the splendid suggestion as outlined in your letter to Mr. Truman which would find a united people offering prayer in the hope that as the holiday season approaches we could at least vision Peace on Earth and Good Will to all Men.

All thinking people are gravely concerned over the ill-advised reply you received from Mr. Truman and yet in the trend of events I doubt if there be reason to expect from this man, who seems to have gone off the beam, and has on several occasions plainly indicated the character of the man. . . . I am at a loss to express in words my feelings over the ill-tempered Truman letter. . . .[66]

On the Supreme Court

The correspondence surrounding one episode concerning members of the Supreme Court goes far to express Mr. Hebert's opinions of that body and one member in particular, Associate Justice, William O. Douglas. The Congressman wrote: [67]

Dear Mr. Chief Justice:

I have reference to the action taken on September 12, 1968, by Justice William O. Douglas granting a stay of execution to preclude the assignment of certain reservists to duty in Vietnam.

It is my understanding that the stay order issued by Justice Douglas on September 12, 1968, was provided telephonically by Justice Douglas to the Clerk of the Court. However, my efforts to obtain a certified copy of the stay order have been unavailing. As a matter of fact, neither the U. S. Department of Justice nor the Office of the General Counsel of the Department of the Army, as of September 18, 1968, had been able to obtain a certified copy of this order.

As you are aware, this case involves 113 Army reservists of the 1002d Combat Support Company presently stationed at Fort Meade, Maryland. These members of this Army reserve unit now on active duty have contended that they have been ordered to active duty illegally.

Accordingly, these reservists instituted suit against the United States Government in Federal Court for the purpose of obtaining a judicial determination that their orders to active duty were illegal and, consequently, required their immediate release from active duty.

The suit brought in United States District Court for the District of Maryland, Civil Docket No. 19734, Morse vs. Boswell, was adjudicated on August 6, 1968, by United States District Judge Frank A. Kaufman, who dismissed the petition of the plaintiff for relief.

Subsequently, this District Court decision was affirmed by the United States Court of Appeals on August 26, 1968.

I am advised that thereafter the attorney for the plaintiffs in this case, contacted both you and Justice Black requesting that a stay order be granted preventing the assignment of these 113 unit members to Vietnam, pending a possible determination by the U. S. Supreme Court to grant certiorari. However, on September 6, 1968, both you and Justice Black denied this request.

Despite the action taken by you and Justice Black, it appears that the petitioners then, on September 12, 1968, contacted Justice Douglas, under somewhat bizarre circumstances, for the purpose of reversing the action taken by you and Justice Black and obtaining a stay order.

The sought-after stay order was then directed by Justice Douglas despite the fact that he, admittedly, because of his location, did not have access to all the pertinent ramifications of the case and despite the fact that he was aware that his colleagues, on earlier deliberations and under presumably more favorable circumstances, had denied such a request.

I have consulted with numerous members of the Bar for the purpose of determining whether, in their judgment, and viewed as the attorney for the petitioners, there remains a substantive legal question concerning the provisions of law and the authority utilized by the President of the United States to order these reservists to active duty. In all of these discussions I have been unable to find any responsible member of the law profession who finds any reasonable basis for questioning the decision rendered by the United States District Court in this matter. This assessment is one obviously shared by the United States Court of Appeals, and apparently also by both you and Justice Black.

Despite this absence of a substantive and unresolved legal issue in the suit brought by these reservists, Justice Douglas none the less issued his stay order.

The Secretary of the Army, by reason of his stay order, is now apparently precluded from utilizing these reservists in the manner calculated to best serve the national interest. Moreover, this stay order has the effect of casting a serious legal cloud over the utilization of thousands of other reservists who have been involuntarily ordered to active duty under the authority provided in Public Law 89-687, as well as all other reservists not presently on active duty.

The issuance of this stay order and the attendant publicity given it has therefore had a demoralizing effect on not only the many thousands of dedicated and loyal reservists who are now serving their country on active duty, but has subjected the entire Reserve program to unnecessary ridicule and embarrassment by inferentially questioning the very essence of its being.

The mischief resulting from this arbitrary and capricious action by Justice Douglas is both incalculable and irreparable. His action has encouraged the filing of numerous similar suits throughout the country by reservists who have been ordered to active duty under the provision of Public Law 89-687. Undoubtedly, these actions now being filed by other reservists have been directly precipitated by the issuance of this stay order and the unfounded hope that such action could ultimately effect their early release from active military service.

Although the authority to grant a stay of execution has been granted to the courts and specifically to each U. S. Supreme Court Justice by statute, it is, as I am certain you will agree, an authority to be used with the utmost discretion and only after the most careful and diligent weighing of the relative equities involved.

The circumstances surrounding the issuance of this stay order, in my view, clearly indicate that Justice Douglas was either unmindful of the implication of his actions, or worse, chose to disregard them entirely. In either event, his issuance of a stay order can therefore only be characterized as being arbitrary and capricious—an action which cannot but adversely affect the already tarnished image of the United States Supreme Court.

Although I presume that shortly after the Court reconvenes on October 7, 1968, it will act quickly to cancel this unfortunate stay order the damage done by Justice Douglas cannot be undone.

In view of these cirmcumstances, you can readily understand my concern that continued indiscriminate and capricious use of this stay order authority may require Congress to legislate on the subject.

I would be reluctant to recommend a legislative proscription of this judicial authority. Therefore, I am impelled to ask whether the Court itself can within its own organization and authority establish rules of procedure which will preclude a repetition of this unfortunate circumstance in the future?

Sincerely yours,
F. Edw. Hebert

Chief Justice Warren replied: [68]

My dear Congressman:

This will acknowledge your letter of September 19th, and advise you that in the regular course of business the case of *Morse* v. *Boswell* will be considered by the entire Court during the first week of the coming Term which commences on October 7th.

Sincerely,
Earl Warren

Once this exchange was made public, Mr. Hebert received a large volume of mail supporting his view as set forth in the letter to the Chief Justice. A judge from California, however, took issue with Hebert, and in his reply Hebert goes further in clarifying his attitude toward the functions of the Supreme Court.

In part, the California judge wrote: [69]

Dear Sir:

While I favor the presence of American troops in Vietnam, I found it incredible that you, as a member of Congress would write to the United States Supreme Court commenting on a matter that was up before the court for decision. This shows a lack of knowledge of our form of government, and the co-equal status of the three departments of our government.

Commenting to a judge on a case pending before the court is regarded as tampering with the judicial process, and is the basis for a contempt of court proceeding. . . .

I continue to find it hard to believe that persons in such high positions as you possess would, in an apparent play for publicity, seek to chastise one of the justices of the United States Supreme Court for allegedly delaying the shipment of reservists to Vietnam. It does not take much courage to attack a judge, because it is unethical for him to hold a news conference and strike back through the news media. . . .

Mr. Hebert replied: [70]

Dear Judge Campbell:

I have your letter of October 14 with reference to my statements pertaining to the stay orders which were issued by Supreme Court Justice William O. Douglas.

Your naivete is most refreshing. I believe so strongly in the three divisions of government as set forth in the Constitution that I almost have a heart attack when the Supreme Court writes the law instead of interpreting it.

I almost have a double heart attack when I see Justices writing books and making speeches on matters which are before the Court and on which they may have to sit in judgment.

If this country had a Supreme Court which observed its functions, I would not be prompted to issue criticisms. And if you think the Justices don't avail themselves of an opportunity to issue statements, then I urge you to look into the matter that storks don't bring babies.

Sincerely yours,
F. Edw. Hebert

On Civil Rights Legislation

The following four letters present some facets of Hebert's attitude toward civil rights legislation.

Dear Mr. Talley:

I certainly thank you very much for your letter and your expressions, and let me say to you that I could not agree with you more, that two wrongs do not make a right.

That is exactly the point I was trying to make in my broadcast about Martin Luther King. Those of us who disagree with these street riots and the antics of Martin Luther King have been told for years to have our recourse in the courts, yet they refuse to obey the orders of the courts.

When the state troopers use tear gas in Alabama, they are criticized. In Mississippi, the Federal Marshals used tear gas but nobody criticized them. In Alabama, and other places in the South where there have been demonstrations and the demonstrators have been dragged out by the police, it is called brutality, but when the demonstrators are dragged out of the White House and the Department of Justice, it was simple arrest.

I think I made it quite clear in my broadcast that this was my position. I have repeated this position time and again, and I stand by it.

I note that you state you supported me the first time I ran for office some twenty-five years ago, which I assure you I appreciate deeply, and I hope I have merited your support since then and will continue to do so.

I believe that the laws of the states, the cities, and the nation should be obeyed by everybody, whether they be white, black, pink or purple.

Sincerely yours,
F. EDWARD HEBERT [71]

Dear Mr. Demmons:

This will acknowledge your telegram of this date addressed to me as Senator Hebert, which, of course, I am not. I am a United States Representative.

I believe in the rights not only of the minorities but also the majorities. I do not concur at all in the President's attempt to destroy the rights of the minorities and the majorities, and I shall oppose any legislation which would take away from individuals their rights and privileges in order to give to others license and abuse.

With kindest regards.

Sincerely yours,
F. EDW. HEBERT [72]

Dear Mr. Russell:

Thank you for your letter of August 23.

You are so right! It is time that the rights of the taxpaying, non-rioting, respectable majority of the voting citizens of this country are protected, and you may rest assured I shall continue to do everything that I can to force the Department of Justice to take this course of action.

With kindest regards.

Sincerely yours,
F. EDW. HEBERT [73]

Dear Miss Sponheim:

Thank you for your letter of March 5 concerning the remedial measures suggested in the recent Riot Commission report.

Whereas I deeply appreciate your interest and receiving your views, in all frankness, I must disagree.

My comment about the Riot Commission report was that it was 'propaganda ad nauseam.' The people who did the rioting and looting were in no way admonished by the Commission, and certainly they should have been. These people who go around the country preaching treasonous and seditious statements and inciting people to riot should be put behind bars.

As for meaningful civil rights legislation, I have consistently opposed so-called civil rights measures. I believe that an individual, regardless of race, color or creed, should have an opportunity to make of himself what he wants to make. And legislation which tries to force unearned favors upon people will not solve the problem.

I don't feel that more handouts is the answer to unrest in our cities. We can't buy peace. We must make these people realize that only through constructive efforts and the ballot box can they achieve their goals. Certainly burning their own homes and businesses is not the solution.

As for a tax increase, I would only vote for one if it was needed for the war effort. As of this time I have not been convinced that a tax increase is needed.

Again, although we disagree in these areas, I do appreciate your making known your views to me. Only through increased interest on the part of citizens and meaningful discussion of the problems can a quicker solution be reached.

With kindest regards.

Sincerely yours,
F. Edw. Hebert [74]

I F ONE TRULY seeks to discover the basis of Hebert's success in his two careers of journalism and politics, then this investigation certainly points in one direction—consistency. But, one might ask, consistency to what? The answer has to be consistency to a set of ideals, to a code of ethics and a sense of practicality that has produced in Hebert a devotion to fair play.

The foregoing investigation points up Hebert's consistency to fundamental American ideals. Ideals that are not superficially interpreted as flag waving or political speech making on the Fourth of July, or platitudinous mouthings on the evening TV newscasts. Hebert's ideals are based squarely on the concept of fair play.

Here, then, is Hebert's strength of character. Here, too, is the source of the Congressman's success. Hebert's sense of fair play is far more important to him on a day-to-day basis than any amount of partisanship or meaningless political rhetoric, for he knows that fair play breeds responsibility, it engenders understanding, and it conceives a willingness to stop shouting and start listening. Hebert knows that with responsibility, understanding and a willingness to listen and learn, there are few problems facing the American nation that cannot be easily swept aside. He is convinced that political labels—Democrat, Republican, liberal, conservative or reactionary—are meaningless in the face of fair play for all Americans. Hebert believes that many American political issues such as black versus white, labor versus management, North versus South,

189

internationalist versus isolationist, and a host of others, quickly evaporate when confronted by a mutual desire for fair play.

At this point in American history when people from nine to ninety are shouting for freedom, Hebert repeatedly emphasizes that real freedom—freedom for the spirit as well as the body—can only build upward from a base of fair play. Throughout his career, the Congressman has demonstrated that such things as racism, mob violence, political quackery, moral license and hate propaganda are but oversized sand castles which are easily undermined and washed away by a tide of fair play.

Devoted to the great ideals of American freedom, Hebert has stood solidly against the concept that real leadership can be found in screaming nationalists, moody pseudo liberals, psychotic demagogues, or selfish egoists. He believes that true leadership can only be founded upon justice.

Hence, for thirty years F. Edward Hebert has faithfully served the people of Louisiana's First Congressional District—the people of Louisiana—indeed, the American nation.

"... it is important that you live for your country, but more important is that you are willing to die for your country."

F. EDWARD HÉBERT, M.C.
June 20, 1970

CHAPTER I

1 Joseph Culotta, Jr. (narrator and producer), "The History of a Man and a Country," on radio program *Let's Talk it Over*. Radio Station WTIX, New Orleans, La., July 28, 1968. Electromagnetic tape.*

* Except for monographs and articles cited, all materials used in the preparation of this work are from the private collection of personal papers relating to the congressional career of F. Edward Hebert (Hereinafter cited as FEH) deposited in his personal library in New Iberia, Louisiana.

The collection contains individual letters; privately bound collections of speeches, without pagination; electromagnetic voice tapes; television and newsreel films. All items are privately cataloged and classified. Those classifications are cited throughout this work.

2 *Ibid.*

3 F. Edward Hebert, *Collected High School Essays and Debates of F. Edward Hebert*. Unpublished manuscripts privately bound.

4 *Ibid.*

5 *New Orleans States*, June 9, 1935, p. 1.

6 *Ibid.*, January 16, 1935, p. 1.

7 *Ibid.*, January 9, 1935, p. 1.

8 F. Edward Hebert, *I Went, I Saw, I Heard* (New Orleans: Franklin Printing Co., Inc., 1945) p. 43.

9 Jo Thompson, "He Makes the Brass See Red," *The Saturday Evening Post*, May 10, 1952, p. 36.

10 Richard M. Nixon, *Six Crises* (New York: Doubleday Publishers, 1962), p. 25.

11 Whittaker Chambers, *Witness* (New York: Random House, 1952), p. 537.

12 Jo Thompson, "He Makes the Brass See Red," *The Saturday Evening Post*, May 10, 1952, p. 36.

13 Radio address by FEH. *Radio Reports, 1947.*

14 Radio program, "Meet the Member." Radio Station WMAL, Washington, D. C., February, 1969.

15 *Eniwetok Scrapbook*

16 *The Times-Picayune*, January 24, 1906, p. 1.

17 *Ibid.*, December 11, 1967, Section 3, p. 18.

193

18 Drew Pearson, "Washington Merry-go-round," *New Orleans States-Item,* November 30, 1967.

19 *New Orleans States-Item,* November 30, 1967, p. 1.

20 *Ibid.,* December 12, 1969, p. 1.

21 *Public Law 90–110,* October 21, 1967.

22 "The History of a Man and a Country." Electromagnetic tape.

23 Address by Hugh M. Wilkinson, President, Louisiana Historical Society, January 3, 1966.

24 *Campaign Brochures, 1946.*

25 "The History of a Man and a Country." Electromagnetic tape.

26 *Ibid.*

27 *Ibid.*

28 *Campaign Brochures, 1946.*

29 *Ibid.*

30 *Ibid.*

31 *Ibid.*

32 *Ibid.*

33 *Ibid.*

34 "The History of a Man and a Country," Electromagnetic tape.

35 *Campaign Brochures, 1946.*

36 Hebert Library, New Iberia, La.

37 *Ibid.*

38 *Ibid.*

39 *Ibid.*

40 *Ibid.*

41 *Ibid.*

42 *Ibid.*

43 *Ibid.*

44 *Ibid.*

45 *Ibid.*

46 First Congressional District Office, New Orleans, Louisiana.

CHAPTER II

1 Radio address by FEH, July 4, 1947. *Radio Talks, 1945–1952.*

2 Radio address by FEH, June 21, 1954, *Radio Talks, 1954.*

3 Speech by FEH, Annual Banquet of the Staff of Baptist Hospital. New Orleans, Louisiana, March 28, 1950. *Radio and Campaign Addresses, 1940–1950.*

4 Radio address by FEH, May 1, 1948. *Radio Talks, 1948.*

5 Radio address by FEH, August 15, 1944. *Radio and Campaign Addresses, 1940-1950.*

6 Speech by FEH before the Past Presidents' Day Luncheon, Young Men's Business Club of New Orleans, Roosevelt Hotel, New Orleans, Louisiana, July 21, 1943. *Radio and Campaign Addresses, 1940-1950.*

7 Radio address by FEH, May 9, 1949. *Radio Addresses, 1949.*

8 Speech by FEH, Annual Banquet of the Staff of Baptist Hospital, New Orleans, Louisiana, March 28, 1950. *Radio and Campaign Addresses, 1940-1950.*

9 Letter to Mrs. Richard A. Koch from FEH, Washington, D. C., July 27, 1961.

10 Radio address by FEH, August 15, 1944. *Radio and Campaign Speeches, 1940-1950.*

11 Radio address by FEH, March 17, 1951. Electromagnetic tape #95.

[12] Radio address by FEH, May 24, 1948. *Radio Talks, 1948.*

[13] Radio address by FEH, March 13, 1950. *Radio Addresses, 1950.*

[14] Radio address by FEH, January 10, 1949. *Radio Addresses, 1949.*

[15] Speech by FEH, Annual Banquet of the Staff of Baptist Hospital, New Orleans, Louisiana, March 28, 1950. *Radio and Campaign Addresses, 1940-1950.*

[16] Radio address by FEH, March 17, 1951. Electromagnetic tape #95.

[17] Radio address by FEH, June 20, 1949. *Radio Addresses, 1949.*

[18] Radio address by FEH, March 13, 1950. *Radio Addresses, 1950.*

[19] Speech by FEH, September 17, 1949. Electromagnetic tape #93.

[20] Radio address by FEH, March 27, 1948. *Radio Talks, 1948.*

[21] Television address by FEH, July 4, 1967. Electromagnetic tape #58.

[22] Speech by FEH to the student body of S. J. Peters High School, September 17, 1958. Electromagnetic tape #6.

[23] Memorial Exercises in the House of Representatives, May 28, 1946. *Radio Talks, 1946.*

[24] Television address by FEH, October 29, 1967. Electromagnetic tape #65.

[25] Statement by FEH, May 10, 1954. *Press Releases, 1944-1949.*

[26] Television address by FEH, November 12, 1967. Electromagnetic Tape #103.

[27] Radio address by FEH, March 21, 1949. *Radio Addresses, 1949.*

[28] Radio address by FEH, undated. *Radio Addresses, 1950.*

[29] Radio address by FEH, March 21, 1949. *Radio Addresses, 1949.*

[30] Radio address by FEH, July 11, 1949. *Radio Addresses, 1949.*

[31] Campaign speech by FEH, July 18, 1950. *Campaign Speeches, 1948 and 1950.*

[32] Radio address by FEH, April 15, 1953. *Radio Reports, 1953.*

[33] Radio address by FEH, June 16, 1954. *Radio Talks, 1954.*

[34] U.S., Congress, House, Speech by F. Edward Hebert on the Floor of the House of Representatives, 90th Cong., 1st sess., May 8, 1967. *Congressional Record*, CXIII, part 9, 11930.

[35] Television address by FEH, November 12, 1967. *Congressional Report, November 12, 1967* (unbound transcript).

[36] Speech by FEH to the student body of Nicholls High School, New Orleans, Louisiana, Spring, 1968. Electromagnetic tape #151.

[37] Radio address by FEH, April 11, 1945. *Radio and Campaign Addresses, 1940-1950.*

[38] Radio address by FEH, July, 1946. *Radio Talks, 1945-1952.*

[39] Radio address by FEH, February 5, 1951. *Radio Addresses, 1951.*

[40] Radio address by FEH, June 7, 1948. *Radio Talks, 1948.*

[41] Radio address by FEH, February 23, 1951. *Radio Addresses, 1951.*

[42] Radio address by FEH, June 4, 1954. *Radio Talks, 1954.*

[43] Radio address by FEH, April 4, 1949. *Radio Addresses, 1949.*

[44] Radio address by FEH, July, 1946. *Radio Talks, 1946-1952.*

[45] Radio address by FEH, (1948?). *Radio Talks, 1948.*

[46] Television address by FEH, February 16, 1969. *Congressional Report, February 16, 1969* (unbound transcript).

[47] Interview with FEH by Ann Corrick, August 23, 1965, for *Washington Viewpoint.* Electromagnetic tape #8.

[48] Remarks by FEH, Chairman of the Special Investigating Subcommittee of the House Armed Services Committee before the American Society of Newspaper Editors on a Discussion Panel of the Right of the Press to know about Legislative Proceedings, April 22, 1955. Press Release, April 22, 1955.

[49] Television address by FEH, October 29, 1967. Electromagnetic tape #65.

[50] Television address by FEH, March 2, 1969. *Congressional Report, March 2, 1969* (unbound transcript).

[51] Speech by FEH, Annual Banquet of the Staff of Baptist Hospital, New Orleans, Louisiana, March 28, 1950. *Radio and Campaign Addresses, 1940-1950.*

[52] Television address by FEH, February 9, 1967. Electromagnetic tape #150.

[53] Interview with FEH by Bill Dickinson, July 26, 1967, Electromagnetic tape #50.

[54] Television address by FEH, June 23, 1968. *Congressional Report, June 23, 1968* (unbound transcript).

[55] Television address by FEH, December 10, 1967. Electromagnetic tape #107.

[56] Television address by FEH, August 6, 1967. *Congressional Report, August 6, 1967* (unbound transcript).

[57] Television address by FEH, May 20, 1967. Electromagnetic tape #47.

[58] Interview with FEH by Bill Dickinson, July 26, 1967. Electromagnetic tape #50.

[59] *Ibid.*

[60] Television address by FEH, April 28, 1968. *Congressional Report, April 28, 1968.* (Unbound transcript).

[61] Radio address by FEH, May 30, 1949. *Radio Addresses, 1949.*

[62] Television address by FEH, June 9, 1968. *Congressional Report, June 9, 1968* (unbound transcript).

[63] Speech by FEH to the student body of Nicholls High School, New Orleans, Louisiana, Spring, 1968. Electromagnetic tape #151.

[64] Television address by FEH, June 9, 1968. Electromagnetic tape #121.

[65] Radio address by FEH, July 4, 1967. Electromagnetic tape #58.

[66] Television address by FEH, April 28, 1968. *Congressional Report, April 28, 1968* (unbound transcript).

[67] Radio address by FEH, 1945. *Radio Talks, 1945-1952.*

CHAPTER III

[1] Radio address by FEH, February 22, 1954. *Radio Talks, 1954.*

[2] Radio address by FEH, June 6, 1946. *Radio Talks, 1945-1952.*

[3] Radio address by FEH, March 22, 1948. *Radio Talks, 1948.*

[4] Radio address by FEH, April 21, 1953. *Radio Reports, 1953.*

[5] Radio address by FEH, June 17, 1953. *Ibid.*

[6] Radio address by FEH, October 21, 1941, (unbound transcript).

[7] Radio address by FEH, undated. *Radio Addresses, 1944-1950.*

[8] F. Edward Hebert, *I Went, I Saw, I Heard* (New Orleans, 1945) p. 45.

[9] Speech by FEH, July 10, 1950. *Campaign Speeches, 1948 and 1950.*

[10] Speech by FEH to the student body of Nicholls High School, New Orleans, Louisiana, Spring, 1968. Electromagnetic Tape #151.

[11] Radio address by FEH, February 10, 1951. *Radio Addresses, 1951.*

[12] *Ibid.*

[13] Television address by FEH, June 25, 1967. Electromagnetic Tape #62.

[14] Speech by FEH before the Past Presidents' Day Luncheon, Young Men's Business Club of New Orleans, Roosevelt Hotel, New Orleans, Louisiana, July 21, 1943. *Radio and Campaign Addresses, 1940-1950.*

[15] Television address by FEH, June 23, 1968. Electromagnetic Tape #123.

[16] Speech by FEH, Annual Banquet of the Staff of Baptist Hospital, New Orleans, Louisiana, March 28, 1950. *Radio and Campaign Addresses, 1940-1950.*

[17] Hebert, *I Went, I Saw, I Heard.* This journal of a trip through Western Europe on the morrow of World War II is replete with compassion for those human beings who were orgiastically butchered and broken by Hitler and his ilk.

[18] Radio address by FEH, May 30, 1946. *Radio Talks, 1945–1952.*

[19] Hebert, *I Went, I Saw, I Heard*, p. 43.

[20] Radio address by FEH, 1946. *Radio Talks, 1946.*

[21] Hebert, *I Went, I Saw, I Heard*, pp. 43–45.

[22] Radio address by FEH, March 22, 1948. *Radio Talks, 1948.*

[23] Radio address by FEH, March 29, 1948. *Ibid.*

[24] Radio address by FEH, February 10, 1951. *Radio Addresses, 1951.*

[25] Hebert, *I Went, I Saw, I Heard*, p. 45.

[26] Radio address by FEH, April 6, 1953. *Radio Reports, 1953.*

[27] Radio address by FEH, 1948. *Miscellaneous Speeches, 1935–1967.*

[28] Radio address by FEH, June 13, 1949. *Radio Addresses, 1949.*

[29] Radio address by FEH, April 11, 1949. *Ibid.*

[30] Hebert, *I Went, I Saw, I Heard*, p. 49.

[31] Radio addresses by FEH, 1948; March, 1948; April 12, 1948. *Radio Talks, 1948.*

[32] Radio address by FEH, February 10, 1954. *Radio Talks, 1954.*

[33] Radio address by FEH, February 1, 1954. *Ibid.*

[34] Radio address by FEH, February 9, 1954. *Ibid.*

[35] *Ibid.*

[36] Radio address by FEH, June 6, 1946. *Radio Talks, 1945–1952.*

[37] Radio address by FEH, July 14, 1953. *Radio Talks, 1953.*

[38] Radio address by FEH, March 24, 1953. *Radio Reports, 1953.*

[39] Radio address by FEH, May 22, 1953. *Radio Talks, 1953.*

[40] *Ibid.*

[41] Radio address by FEH, July 14, 1953. *Ibid.*

[42] Radio address by FEH, May 22, 1953. *Ibid.*

[43] Radio address by FEH, March 31, 1954. *Radio Talks, 1954.*

[44] Speech by FEH, July 19, 1950. *Campaign Speeches, 1948–1950.*

[45] *Ibid.*

[46] Radio address by FEH, April 13, 1953. *Radio Reports, 1953.*

[47] Radio address by FEH, July 20, 1953. *Radio Talks, 1953.*

[48] Radio address by FEH, March 25, 1953. *Ibid.*

[49] Radio address by FEH, May 13, 1953. *Ibid.*

[50] Radio address by FEH, February 9, 1954. *Radio Talks, 1954.* Anyone who has followed the Vietnam conflict with any knowledge of how this country became involved will recall that President Eisenhower, in 1959, committed the technical advisors to assist the South Vietnamese.

[51] Radio address by FEH, February 15, 1954. *Ibid.*

[52] Radio address by FEH, April 15, 1954. *Ibid.*

[53] *Ibid.*

[54] Radio address by FEH, April 27, 1954. *Ibid.*

[55] Radio address by FEH, May 4, 1954. *Ibid.*

[56] *Ibid.* The last paragraph of this statement is indeed interesting in view of the fact that it was not until the Nixon Administration that Washington politicians seriously began talking about the Vietnamization of the war.

[57] Radio address by FEH, May 10, 1954. *Ibid.*

[58] Radio address by FEH, June 2, 1954. *Ibid.*

[59] Radio address by FEH, June 7, 1954. *Ibid.*

[60] Radio address by FEH, June 25, 1954. *Ibid.*

61 *Ibid.*

62 Television address by FEH, February 5, 1966. Film #120.

63 U.S., Congress, House, Speech by F. Edward Hebert on the Floor of the House of Representatives, 90th Cong., 1st sess., May 8, 1967. *Congressional Record*, CXIII, Part 9, 11930.

64 Television address by FEH, February 5, 1966. Film #120.

65 Television address by FEH, December 14, 1967. Electromagnetic Tape #148.

66 Television address by FEH, December 10, 1967. Electromagnetic Tape #107.

67 Interview of FEH by Bill Dickinson, March 20, 1968. Electromagnetic Tape #83.

68 *Ibid.*

69 Television address by FEH, undated. Film #126.

70 *Ibid.*

71 *Ibid.*

72 Television address by FEH, February 5, 1966. Film #120.

73 Television address by FEH, June 25, 1967. Electromagnetic Tape #62.

CHAPTER IV

1 Radio address by FEH, July 3, 1941 (unbound transcript).

2 *Ibid.*

3 Speech by FEH before the Past President's Day Luncheon, Young Men's Business Club of New Orleans, Roosevelt Hotel, New Orleans, Louisiana, July 21, 1943. *Radio and Campaign Addresses, 1940–1950.*

4 Radio address by FEH, undated. *Radio Talks, 1954.*

5 Letter to the Editor, *The Times-Picayune*, from FEH, Washington, D. C., December 24, 1951.

6 Speech by FEH before the Past Presidents' Day Luncheon, Young Men's Business Club of New Orleans, Roosevelt Hotel, New Orleans, Louisiana, July 21, 1943. *Radio and Campaign Addresses, 1940–1950.*

7 Interview of FEH by Ann Corrick for *Washington Viewpoint*, August 23, 1965. Electromagnetic Tape #8.

8 Radio address by FEH, 1945. *Radio Talks, 1945–1952.*

9 Radio address by FEH, June 6, 1953. *Radio Reports, 1953.*

10 Radio address by FEH, June 23, 1954. *Radio Talks, 1954.*

11 Remarks by FEH, Chairman of the Special Investigating Subcommittee of the House Armed Services Committee before the American Society of Newspaper Editors on a Discussion Panel of the Right of the Press to know about Legislative Proceedings, April 22, 1955. *Press Release, April 22, 1955.*

12 Address by FEH before the Harvard University Forum, Cambridge, Mass., February 11, 1949. *Miscellaneous Speeches, 1935–1967.*

13 Radio address by FEH, March 23, 1954. *Radio Talks, 1954.*

14 Radio address by FEH, March 19, 1954. *Ibid.*

15 Radio address by FEH, April 14, 1954. *Ibid.*

16 Remarks by FEH, Chairman of the Special Investigating Subcommittee of the House Armed Services Committee before the American Society of Newspaper Editors on a Discussion Panel of the Right of the Press to know about Legislative Proceedings, April 22, 1955. *Press Release, April 22, 1955.*

17 Letter to Rolfe H. McCollister from FEH, Washington, D. C., July 3, 1957.

18 Radio address by FEH, April 10, 1950. *Radio and Campaign Addresses, 1940-1950.*

[19] Radio address by FEH, March 15, 1954. *Radio Talks, 1954.*

[20] Letter to Governor Thomas E. Dewey from FEH, Washington, D. C., September 13, 1958.

[21] Radio address by FEH, February 3, 1954. *Radio Talks, 1954.*

[22] Radio address by FEH, March 10, 1954. *Ibid.*

[23] Radio address by FEH, 1946. *Radio Talks, 1946.*

[24] Radio address by FEH, April 26, 1954. *Radio Talks, 1954*

[25] Interview of FEH for *Capitol Cloakroom*, September 22, 1948. Electromagnetic Tape #87.

[26] Television address by FEH, (1961?). Film #96.

[27] Interview of FEH for *Capitol Cloakroom*, September 22, 1948. Electromagnetic Tape #87.

[28] Radio address by FEH, February 6, 1953. *Radio Reports, 1953.*

The reader will recall that the subject of the objectivity of the mass media was made an issue of some importance after the noteworthy speech of Vice President Spiro Agnew in Des Moines, Iowa, November 7, 1969.

[29] U.S., Congress, House, Extension of Remarks by F. Edward Hebert, "An Open Letter to Raymond Clapper and All Newspaper Reporters and Columnists and Radio Commentators Who Will Cover the New Congress." 78th Cong., 1st sess., January 22, 1943. *Congressional Record Appendix*, LXXXIX, Part 9, A277.

[30] Radio address by FEH, April 16, 1953. *Radio Reports, 1953.*

[31] Radio address by FEH, (approximately 1947). *Radio Talks, 1945-1952.*

[32] *Ibid.*

[33] U.S., Congress, House, Representative F. Edward Hebert speaking on "Freedom of Speech," 78th Cong., 2nd sess., April 12, 1944, *Congressional Record*, XC, 3422.

[34] U.S., Congress, House, Extension of remarks by Representative F. Edward Hebert in the form of "An Open Letter to Raymond Clapper. . . ." 78th Cong., 1st sess., January 22, 1943. *Congressional Record Appendix*, LXXXIX, Part 9, A277.

[35] Letter to Don Robinson, editor, *The American Press*, from FEH, Washington, D. C., April 16, 1947.

[36] Letter to Gould Lincoln from FEH, Washington, D. C., May 20, 1942.

[37] Radio address by FEH, 1945. *Radio Talks, 1945-1952.*

[38] *Ibid.*

[39] *Ibid.*

[40] *Ibid.*

[41] Speech by FEH, August 30, 1948. *Campaign Speeches, 1948 and 1950.*

[42] Radio address by FEH, April 24, 1950. *Radio Addresses, 1950.*

[43] Letter to J. W. Moore from FEH, Washington, D. C., July 25, 1949.

[44] Radio address by FEH, April 24, 1950. *Radio Addresses, 1950.*

[45] Speech by FEH, July 11, 1950. *Miscellaneous Speeches, 1935-1967.*

[46] Speech by FEH, July 14, 1950. *Campaign Speeches, 1948 and 1950.*

[47] Speech by FEH, Annual Banquet of the Staff of Baptist Hospital, New Orleans, Louisiana, March 28, 1950. *Radio and Campaign Addresses, 1940-1950.*

[48] Statement by FEH, August 30, 1956. *Press Releases, 1944-1959.*

[49] Letter to Joseph H. Simpson from FEH, Washington, D. C., November 12, 1964.

[50] Television address by FEH, February 2, 1969. *Congressional Report, February 2, 1969* (unbound transcript).

[51] Radio address by FEH, April 10, 1950. *Radio Talks, 1950.*

[52] Radio address by FEH, February 16, 1954. *Radio Talks, 1954.*

[53] Television address by FEH, February 9, 1967. Electromagnetic Tape #150.

[54] Radio address by FEH, August 5, 1953. *Radio Talks, 1953.*

[55] Letter to President Harry S. Truman from FEH, Washington, D. C., December 5, 1950.

[56] Letter to Congressman F. Edward Hebert from President Harry S. Truman, Washington, D. C., December 7, 1950.

[57] Radio address by FEH, July 14, 1952. *Press Releases, 1944–1959.*

[58] Radio address by FEH, February 23, 1953. *Radio Reports, 1953.* If one will pause to reflect a moment, the statement made in 1953 was generally applicable to 1968.

[59] Radio address by FEH, January 10, 1949. *Radio Addresses, 1949.*

[60] Radio address by FEH, February 14, 1949. *Ibid.*

[61] Radio address by FEH, March 28, 1949. *Ibid.*

[62] Radio address by FEH, May 3, 1949. *Ibid.*

[63] Radio address by FEH, March 17, 1951. Electromagnetic Tape #95.

[64] Radio address by FEH, April 16, 1951. *Radio Addresses, 1951.*

[65] *Ibid.*

[66] Letter to Mr. Jimmie Appel from FEH, Washington, D. C., April 16, 1951.

[67] Radio address by FEH, April 16, 1951. *Radio Addresses, 1951.*

[68] Radio address by FEH, February 26, 1951. *Ibid.*

[69] Radio address by FEH, February 5, 1951. *Ibid.*

[70] Radio address by FEH, January 12, 1953. *Radio Reports, 1953.*

[71] Radio address by FEH, January 21, 1953. *Ibid.*

[72] Radio address by FEH, March 12, 1953. *Ibid.*

[73] Radio address by FEH, August 3, 1953. *Ibid.*

[74] Radio address by FEH, January 19, 1953. *Ibid.*

[75] Radio address by FEH, May 17, 1954. *Radio Talks, 1954.*

[76] Radio address by FEH, June 15, 1954. *Ibid.*

[77] Television address by FEH, August 20, 1967. Electromagnetic Tape #54.

[78] Radio address by FEH, February 14, 1949. *Radio Addresses, 1949.*

[79] Radio Address by FEH, June 27, 1949. *Ibid.*

[80] FEH in panel discussion on "CBS Debate on the Poll Tax," November 6, 1945. *Radio and Campaign Addresses, 1940–1950.*

[81] Radio address by FEH, July 15, 1953. *Radio Talks, 1953.*

[82] Radio address by FEH, February 25, 1954. *Radio Talks, 1954.*

[83] Radio address by FEH, March 14, 1949. *Radio Addresses, 1949.*

[84] U.S., Congress, House, Extension of Remarks by Representative F. Edward Hebert on the subject of "Armed Services Medical Academy," 87th Cong., 1st sess., February 20, 1961. *Congressional Record,* CVII, Part 2, 2477.

[85] Television address by FEH, undated. Film #42.

[86] Television address by FEH, undated (1964?). Film #43.

[87] Television address by FEH, (February, 1964). Film #49.

[88] Television address by FEH, undated (1964?). Film #43.

[89] Television address by FEH, undated (1964?). Film #89.

[90] Letter to Charles F. Weaver from FEH, Washington, D. C., March 12, 1965.

[91] Television address by FEH, undated (1964?). Film #89

[92] Television address by FEH, April 16, 1967. Electromagnetic Tape #45.

[93] Radio address by FEH, 1946. *Radio Talks, 1945–1952.*

[94] Radio address by FEH, June 6, 1946. *Radio Talks, 1946.*

[95] Letter to E. J. Bowen from FEH, Washington, D. C., December 1, 1948.

[96] Speech by FEH, July 18, 1950. *Campaign Speeches 1948 and 1950.*

[97] Radio address by FEH, April 12, 1946. *Radio Talks, 1946.*

⁹⁸ Radio address by FEH (*circa* 1948). *Radio Talks, 1945–1952.*

⁹⁹ *Ibid.*

¹⁰⁰ Television address by FEH, March 2, 1969. *Congressional Report, March 2, 1969* (unbound transcript).

¹⁰¹ Letter to Bill Monroe from FEH, Washington, D. C., February 2, 1950.

¹⁰² Radio address by FEH, January 28, 1954. *Radio Talks, 1954.*

¹⁰³ Radio address by FEH (*circa* 1946). *Radio Talks, 1945–1952.*

¹⁰⁴ Television address by FEH, June 25, 1967. *Congressional Report, June 25, 1967* (unbound transcript).

¹⁰⁵ Letter to H. S. Riecke, Jr. from FEH, Washington, D. C., March 5, 1965.

¹⁰⁶ Letter to Mr. and Mrs. Edward Smira from FEH, Washington, D. C., February 9, 1968.

¹⁰⁷ Radio address by FEH, April, 1946. *Radio Talks, 1945–1952.*

CHAPTER V

¹ Letter to FEH from Fred Lake, New Orleans, Louisiana, May 5, 1967.

² Letter to Fred Lake from FEH, Washington, D. C., May 15, 1967.

³ Letter to FEH from Donald P. Hebert, New Iberia, Louisiana, May 23, 1967.

⁴ Letter to Donald P. Hebert from FEH, Washington, D. C., May 25, 1967.

⁵ Letter to FEH from C. C. Dejoie, Jr., New Orleans, Louisiana, April 8, 1949.

⁶ Letter to C. C. Dejoie, Jr. from FEH, Washington, D. C., April 11, 1949.

⁷ Letter to FEH from F. Winter Trapolin, New Orleans, Louisiana, October 5, 1962.

⁸ Letter to F. Winter Trapolin from FEH, Washington, D. C., October 12, 1962.

⁹ Letter to FEH from Juanita Smith, New Orleans, Louisiana, April 8, 1968.

¹⁰ Letter to Juanita Smith from FEH, Washington, D. C., April 16, 1968 .

¹¹ Letter to FEH from Virgil Keefer, New Orleans, Louisiana, April 7, 1968.

¹² Letter to Virgil Keefer from FEH, Washington, D. C., April 17, 1968.

¹³ Letter to FEH from Mrs. A. J. Canale, New Orleans, Louisiana, April 8, 1968.

¹⁴ Letter to Mrs. A. J. Canale from FEH, Washington, D. C., April 10, 1968.

¹⁵ Letter to FEH from F. Otway Denny, New Orleans, Louisiana, April 12, 1968.

¹⁶ Letter to F. Otway Denny from FEH, Washington, D. C., April 15, 1968.

¹⁷ Letter to Lloyd L. Drury from FEH, Washington, D. C., July 17, 1967.

¹⁸ Letter to FEH from A. J. Frey, New Orleans, Louisiana, November 9, 1965.

¹⁹ Letter to A. J. Frey from FEH, Washington, D. C., November 11, 1965.

²⁰ Letter to FEH from John P. Dodd, New Orleans, Louisiana, April 24, 1967.

²¹ Letter to John P. Dodd from FEH, Washington, D. C., April 27, 1967.

²² Letter to Mrs. F. Robert Mendow from FEH, Washington, D. C., January 23, 1968.

²³ Letter to FEH from Brother Wilbur, New Orleans, Louisiana, March 27, 1968.

²⁴ Letter to Brother Wilbur from FEH, Washington, D. C., March 29, 1968.

²⁵ Letter to FEH from John Schwegmann, Jr., New Orleans, Louisiana, August 8, 1967.

²⁶ Letter to John Schwegmann, Jr. from FEH, Washington, D. C., August 16, 1967.

²⁷ Letter to FEH from F. K. McNeel, Metairie, Louisiana, March 5, 1968.

[28] Letter to F. K. McNeel from FEH, Washington, D. C., March 12, 1968.

[29] Letter to FEH from Albert Cutrer, New Orleans, Louisiana, October 31, 1968.

[30] Letter to Albert Cutrer from FEH, Washington, D. C., November 5, 1968.

[31] Letter to FEH from Dr. Merrill Hines, New Orleans, Louisiana, June 14, 1968.

[32] Letter to Dr. Merrill Hines from FEH, Washington, D. C., June 18, 1968.

[33] Letter to R. J. Meers from FEH, Washington, D. C., June 27, 1968.

[34] Letter to Richard B. Geldert from FEH, Washington, D. C., November 7, 1967.

[35] Letter to FEH from Mrs. Loretta L. Bickerstaff, New Orleans, Louisiana, October 18, 1967.

[36] Letter to Mrs. Loretta L. Bickerstaff from FEH, Washington, D. C., October 23, 1967.

[37] Letter to C. D. Byers from FEH, Washington, D. C., May 13, 1968.

[38] Letter to FEH from R. Richardson King, New Orleans, Louisiana, June 14, 1968.

[39] Letter to R. Richardson King from FEH, Washington, D. C., June 19, 1968.

[40] Letter to Mr. Edward M. Boutte, Jr. from FEH, Washington, D. C., December 13, 1950.

[41] Letter to Secretary of State James F. Byrnes from FEH, Washington, D. C., February 4, 1946.

[42] Letter to FEH from Secretary of State James F. Byrnes, Washington, D. C., February 6, 1946.

[43] Letter to Miss Myra Mier from FEH, Washington, D. C., March 11, 1968.

[44] Letter to Ralph M. Pons from FEH, Washington, D. C., August 16, 1965.

[45] Letter to Edward Lee Tharp from FEH, Washington, D. C., October 21, 1966.

[46] Letter to William W. Westbrook from FEH, Washington, D. C., March 17, 1966.

[47] Letter to Deborah Daugherty from FEH, Washington, D. C., May 15, 1967.

[48] Letter to Mr. and Mrs. M. T. Haddock from FEH, Washington, D. C., March 28, 1968.

[49] Letter to William Storek from FEH, Washington, D. C., June 24, 1941.

[50] Letter to J. E. Connell from FEH, Washington, D. C., March 4, 1949.

[51] Letter to FEH from Gerard F. Schiappa, Washington, D. C., May 16, 1967.

[52] Letter to Gerard F. Schiappa from FEH, Washington, D. C., May 17, 1967.

[53] Letter to FEH from Arnold Klein, Baton Rouge, Louisiana, June 30, 1946.

[54] Letter to Arnold Klein from FEH, Washington, D. C., July 12, 1946.

[55] Letter to Gerald H. Schreiber from FEH, New Orleans, Louisiana, December 23, 1964.

[56] Letter to Kate Herbert from FEH, Washington, D. C., March 12, 1968.

[57] Letter to David R. McGuire, Jr., from FEH, Washington, D. C., March 1, 1950.

[58] Letter to President Harry S. Truman from FEH, Washington, D. C., December 5, 1950.

[59] Letter to FEH from President Harry S. Truman, Washington, D. C., December 7, 1950.

[60] Letter to FEH from Mark Dwire, Shelby, Montana, December 14, 1950.

[61] Letter to FEH from Titus Lloyd Crasto, New Orleans, Louisiana, December 13, 1950.

[62] Letter to FEH from Louis D. Carroll, Baltimore, Maryland, December 14, 1950.

[63] Letter to FEH from George W. Campbell, Hazardville, Connecticut, December 12, 1950.

[64] Letter to FEH from Kathryn Bernard, New Lisbon, Wisconsin, December 30, 1950.

[65] Letter to FEH from De Moss Bowers, Santa Monica, California, December 15, 1950.

[66] Letter to FEH from J. Well Gates, Wittenberg, Wisconsin, December 14, 1950.

[67] Letter to Chief Justice Earl Warren from FEH, Washington, D. C., September 19, 1968.

[68] Letter to FEH from Chief Justice Earl Warren, Washington, D. C., September 23, 1968.

[69] Letter to FEH from Judge Gordon Campbell, Salinas, California, October 14, 1968.

[70] Letter to Judge Gordon Campbell from FEH, Washington, D. C., October 18, 1968.

[71] Letter to Joseph Talley from FEH, Washington, D. C., March 19, 1965.

[72] Letter to Robert Demmons from FEH, Washington, D. C., March 16, 1965.

[73] Letter to Robert Russell from FEH, Washington, D. C., August 30, 1967.

[74] Letter to Miss Susan C. Sponheim from FEH, Washington, D. C., March 8, 1968.

PF is an abbreviation for picture folio